# A Gorgeous Gallery

## of Gallant Inventions

## 1578

Scolar Press

1972

SBN 85417 682 9

*Printed in Great Britain by*
*The Scolar Press Limited*
*Menston, Yorkshire, England*

## NOTE

The *Gorgious Gallery* was one of the less popular Elizabethan miscellanies, and seems to have achieved only one edition, in 1578. It was published by Richard Jones, who was undoubtedly spurred on by the extraordinary popularity of *The Paradyse of Daynty Deuices* which had begun its long life two years before, and which the title page of the *Gallery* cunningly recalls, describing the following anthology as 'Garnished and decked with diuers dayntie deuises'. Jones made a more substantial attempt to ensure the popularity of the *Gallery* by authorising considerable borrowing from his earlier and very successful publication, a ballad collection chiefly put together by Clement Robinson and probably printed in 1566, but now surviving other than fragmentarily only in a later form, *A Handefull of Pleasant Delites* (1584). The compilers of the *Gallery* were Thomas Proctor, whose initials appear on the title page, and Owen Roydon, who wrote a defensive poem to introduce the collection. Roydon seems to have begun the work and Proctor possibly took it over at sig. K4 (where the running-title is interrupted to allow the first explicit appearance of his name); Proctor also, no doubt, gave the miscellany its final form. A[nthony] M[unday], Proctor's friend and at the time probably fellow-apprentice in John Allde's printing shop, contributed puffing verses.

The poems here 'ioyned together and builded up' include contributions by Roydon and Proctor, as well as by such men as Lord Vaux the elder, Thomas Churchyard, Thomas Howell, Clement Robinson and Jasper Heywood. There is nothing very startling about the collection, except perhaps its very great number of different metrical forms, but it is pleasant in a low-keyed, conventional and sententious way: '*respice finem*, a vew of vayn glory, a louers lyfe'. Hyder Rollins sums up the matter: 'although the *Gorgeous Gallery* says little that is new, it does reflect faithfully the sentiments and ideas of Tottel's *Miscellany*, the *Handful*, and the *Paradise*. It holds up a mirror to the age that directly preceded Shakespeare. The *Gorgeous Gallery* came ten or fifteen years too late: in 1565, or even in 1576, it would undoubtedly have been a 'best seller'; in 1578 it was thrown into a vain competition with the serious, courtly poems of the *Paradise*.'

Malone's copy of the *Gallery*, long mistakenly thought to be imperfect, is reproduced here (original size) by permission of the curators of the Bodleian Library (shelf-mark: Mal. 464a).

*Reference:* STC. 20402; *A Gorgeous Gallery of Gallant Inventions* (1578), edit. by H. E. Rollins, 1926.

D. E. L.CRANE

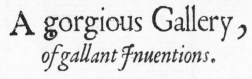

A gorgious Gallery,
*of gallant Inuentions.*

Garniſhed and decked with
*diuers dayntie deuiſes, right*
Delicate and delightfull, to re=
create eche modeſt minde
withall.

Firſt framed and faſhioned in
ſundrie formes, by Diuers worthy
workemen of late dayes : and now,
ioyned together and
builded vp :

By  T. P.

¶ Imprinted at London,
*for Richard Iones.*
1578.

# A. M. Vnto all yong Gentilmen,

## in commendacion of this Gallery
### and workemen therof.

EE Gallaunts, see, this Gallery of delightes,
With buyldings braue, imbost of variant hue :
With daynties deckt, deuisde by worthy wights,
(Which) as time serude, vnto perfection grew.
By studies toyle with phrases fine they fraught :
This peereles peece, filde full, of pretty pith :
And trimde it, (with) what skill, and learning taught,
In hope to please your longing mindes therwith.
Which workemanship, by worthy workemen wrought,
(Perusde) least in obliuion it should ly :
A willing minde, eche part togeather sought,
And termde (the whole) A gorgious Gallerye :
Wherin you may, to recreate the minde,
Such fyne Inuentions finde, for your delight :
That, for desart, their dooings will you binde,
To yeelde them prayse, so well a worke to wright.

### FINIS. A. M.

# Owen Roydon to the curious
## company of Sycophantes.

He busie Bees whose paynes doo neuer misse,
But toyle their time the winters want to wielde :
And heape in hiues, the thing that needfull is,
To feede their flocke till winter bee exilde :
Somtimes the *Drones* the Hony combes doo eate,
And so the Bees must starue for want of meate.

The

# To curious Sycophantes.

The drowsie Drones doo neuer take such toyle,
But lye at lurch, like men of Momus minde :
VVho rudely read and rashly put to foyle,
VVhat worthy workes, so euer they doo finde :
 VVhich workes would please the learned sorte full well,
 But sicophantes will neuer cease to swell.
Though (learnedly) themselues be voyde to write,
And haue not knowen the height of Hellicon :
Yet, carpingly, they needes must spit their spite,
Or els their former force, (they iudge) is gon :
 VVho only liue, the seelly Bees t'annoy,
 And eate the meate, wheron the Bees should ioy.
(Depart from hence) that cursed kinde of crew,
And let this Booke, embrace his earned meede :
VVhich was set forth (for others) not for you,
VVhat likes them best, that only for to reade :
 And let the rest, without rebuke to passe,
 And helpe t'amend the thing that blamelesse was.
(APPELLES) might suffise, to warne you wel,
(who) while hee was a paynting in his Shop :
Came in (a Sowter) who began to swell,
And viewd his Image all from toe to top :
 And scofte at this, and did mislike at that,
 Of many a fault the Champion gan to chat.
At length (Appelles) angry with his man,
Dislyked much and gaue him answere so :
(Talke thou of that, wherin some skill thou can)
Vnto the slipper (Sowter) only go :
 The saucye (Sowter) was abashed much,
 And afterward, his talke was nothing such.
So? (Momus thou) no further then thy marke,
And talke no more, then skill doth giue thee leaue :
But in thy hart, there is a burning sparke,
And (whiles thou liues) that sickenesse will thee greaue :
 But doo thy worst, and doo no more but right,
 The learned route, wil laughe at thy despight.

## FINIS. O. R.

# THE GALLERY
## *of gallant Inuentions.*

To a Gentilwoman that sayd : All men be false,
*they thinke not what they say.*

 Ome women fayne that Paris was,
The falsest louer that could bée :
Who for his (life) did nothing passe,
As all the world might playnly sée :
　But ventred life and limmes and all,
　To kéepe his fréend from Greekish thrall :
　With many a broyle bée dearely bought,
　His (Hellen) whom hée long had sought.
For first (Dame Venus) graunted him,
A gallant gifte of Beauties fléece :
Which boldely for to séeke to win,
By surging Seas hée sayld to Gréece :
　And when hée was arriued theare,
　By earnest sute to win his Deare :
　No greater paynes might man endure,
　Then Paris did, for Hellen sure.
Besides all this when they were well,
Both hée, and shée, arryur'd at Troy :
Kinge Menelaus wrath did swell,
And swore, by sword, to rid their ioyes :
　And so hée did for ten yeres space,
　Hée lay before the Troyans face :
　With all the hoste that hée could make,
　To bée reueng'd for Hellens sake.

A iij　　　　　　　Loe

Loe? thus much did poore Paris bide,
Who is accounted most vntrue :
All men bee false it hath bin sayd,
They thinke not what they speake (say you)
  Yes Paris spoke, and sped with spæde,
  As all the heauenly Gods decræd :
  And proud himselfe a Louer iust,
  Till stately Troy was turnd to dust :
I doo not reade of any man,
That so much was vnfaythfull found :
You did vs wrong, t'accuse vs than,
And say our frændship is not sound :
  If any fault bæ found at all,
  To womens lot it nædes must fall :
  If (Hellen) had not bin so light,
  Sir Paris had not died in fight.
The falsest men I can excuse,
That euer you in stories reade :
Therfore all men for to accuse,
Mæ thinkes it was not well decræde :
  It is a signe you haue not tride,
  What stedfastnesse in men doth bide :
  But when your time shal try them true,
  This iudgment then, you must renue.
I know not euery mans deuise,
But commonly they stedfast are :
Though you doo make them of no price,
They breake their vowes but very rare :
  They will performe theyr promis well,
  And specially where loue doth dwell :
  Where frændship doth not iustly frame,
  Then men (forsooth) must beare the blame.

FINIS.    O. R,

## The lamentable louer abiding in the
### bitter bale of direfull doubts towards
his Ladyes loyalty, writeth vnto her as followeth.

HEalth I thée send, if hée may giue, ý which himself doth misse:
  For thy swéet brest, doth harbor whole, my bloody bale or blisse,
I néede no scribe, to scry my care, in restlesse rigor spread:
They that behold, my chaunged cheare, already iudge mée dead.
My baned limmes, haue yélded vp, their woented ioy to dye:
My healthles hand, doth nought but wring, & dry my dropping eye,
The deadly day, in dole I passe, a thousand times I craue
The noysome night: agayne I wish, the dolefull day to haue.
Eche howre to mée, most hatefull is, eche place doth vrge my wo:
No foode mée féedes, close vp mine eyes, to gastly graue I go.
No Phisickes art, can giue the salue, to heale my paynfull part:
Saue only thou, the salue and sore, of this my captiue hart,
Thou art the branch ý swétly springs, whose hart is sound & true
Can only cheare mée wofull wight, or force my want to rue.
Then giue to mée, the sap I thirste, which gift may giue mée ioy,
I mean thy firme, & faythful loue, whose want bréds mine annoy,
Remember yet sure fréndship had, ypast betwéene vs twayne
Forget him not, for loue of thee, who sighes in secret payne.
I oft doo séeme in company, a gladsome face to beare,
But God thou knowst my inward woes, & cares ý rent mée there:
And that I may, gush out my gréefe, in secret place alone,
I bid my frænds fare well in haste, I say I must be gone.
Then haste I fast, with heauy hart, in this my dolefull case:
Where walkes no wight, but I alone, in drowsie desart place,
And there I empt, my laden hart, that sweld in fretting mone:
My sighes and playnts, and panges I tell, vnto my selfe alone.
What shall I say? doo aske mée once, why all these sorowes bee?
I answere true, O foe or freend, they all are made for thee.

                       Once

Once knit the lynck,that loue may laſt,then ſhal my dollors ceaſſ
It lyes in thee,and wilt thou not, the yeelding wight releaſe?
O would to God,it lay in mæ,to cure ſuch græfe of thine: (mine,
Thou ſhouldſt not long,be voyd of helpe, if twere in power of
But I would run,& range in ſtormes,a thouſand miles in payne:
Not fearing foyle,of frænds to haue,my coūtenance whole agayn
And wilt thou then,all mercyleſſe,more longer torment mæ?
In drawing backe,ſith my good helpe,is only whole in thæ?
Then ſend mæ cloſe,ỹ hewing knife,my wider wound to ſcratch;
And thou ſhalt ſæ, by wofull græfe,of life a cleane diſpatch.
When thou ſhalt ſay,and proue it true,my hart entirely lou'd,
Which loſt the life,for counthauce ſwæt frō whō bæ neuer mou'd
Write then vpon my wofull Tombe,theſe verſes grauen aboue,
Heere lyes the hart, his truth to trie, that loſt his life in loue.
Loe,ſaue or ſpill,thou mayſt mee now,thou ſitſt in iudgment hie,
Where I poore man,at Bar doo ſtand,and lowd,for life doo cry.
Thou wilt not bæ,ſo mercyleſſe,to ſlea a louing hart:
Small prayſe it is to conquer him,that durſt no where to ſtart,
Thou haſt the ſword,that cut the wound,of my vnholpen payne:
Thou canſt and art,the only helpe,to heale the ſame agáyne.
Then heale the hart, that loues thæ well,vntill the day bæ dye:
And firmely faſt thy loue on him, thats true continually,
In thæ my wealth,in thee my woe,in thæ to ſaue or ſpill:
In thee mee lyfe,in thee my death,doth reſt to worke thy will.
Let vertue myrt,with pitty great,and louing mercy ſaue
Him,who without thy ſalue,ſo ſicke,that hee muſt yeeld to graue,
O ſalue thou then,my ſecret ſore, ſith health in thee doth ſtay:
And graūt tō ſpeed,my iuſt requeſt, whoſe want works my decay
Then ſhal I bleſſe,the pleaſāt place,where once I toke thy gloue,
And thanke ỹ God,who giues thæ grace,to graūt me loue for loue.

FINIS.

# ¶ A louing Epistle, written by *Ruphilus* a yonge Gentilman, to his best beloued Lady Elriza, as followeth.

Wice hath my quaking hand withdrawen this pen away
And twice againe it gladly would, before I dare bewray
The secret shrined thoughts, that in my hart do dwell,
That neuer wight as yet hath wist, nor I desire to tell.
But as the smothered cole, doth wast and still consume,
And outwardly doth geue no heate, of burnyng blaze or fume:
So hath my hidden harmes, been harbred in my corpce,
Till faintyng limmes and life and all, had welnigh lost his force:
Yet stand I halfe in doubt, whiche of these two to chose,
To hide my harmes still to my hurt, or els this thraldome lose.
I will lay feare aside, and so my tale beginne:
Who neuer durst assaile his foe: did neuer conquest win.
    Lo here my cause of care to thee vnfolde I will:
Help thou Minerua, graunt I pray, some of thy learned skill.
Help all you Muses nine, my wofull Pen to write:
So stuffe my verse with pleasant wordes, as she may haue delight,
With heedyng eares to reade my greif and great vnrest:
Some wordes of plaint may moue perhaps, to pitty my request.
Oft haue I hard complaint, how Cupid beares a sway
In brittle youth, and would commaund: and how they did obay.
When I with skorning eares did all their talke dispise:
But well I see the blinded boy: in lurking den hee lies,
To catch the careles sorte: awayting with his Darte:
Hee threw at mee when I vnwares, was wounded to the harte.
To speake and pray for helpe, now loue hath mee constrainde:
And makes mee yeeld to serue the sorte, that lately I disdainde.
Sith beggars haue no choyce: nor neede had euer law
The subiecte Oxe doth like his yoke: when hee is driuen to draw.
That Ruphilus this wrote: thou wonder wilt I know,
Cause neuer erst in louinge vearse: my labor I bestowe,
Well, woful loue is mine, and weeping lines I wright,
And doubtfull wordes with driery cheere: beseemes a careful wight
O thou Elrisa fayre, the beuty of thine eyes
Hath bred such bale within my brest, and cau'sde such strife to ryse.

As I can not forget : vntill deuouring death
Shal leaue to mæ a senceles goast : and rid my longer breath,
Or at the least that thou : do graunt mæ some relæfe
To ease the grædy gripes I fæle, and end my great mischæfe.
As due to mæ by right, I can no mercy craue,
Thou hast the power to graunt mæ life : refuse not for to saue.
Put to thy helping hand, to salue the wounded sore,
Though thou refuse it for my sake : yet make thine honour more,
To cruell were the facte : if thou shouldst sæke to kill
Thy faythful frænd that loues thee so : and doth demaund no ill.
Thy heauenly shape I saw : thy passing bewty bright,
Enforst mæ to assay the bayt : where now my bane I bight
I nought repent my loue : nor yet forthinke my facte,
The Gods I know were all agræd : and secretly compacte.
To frame a worke of prayse : to show their power deuine
By good aduice this on the earth : aboue the rest to shine.
Whose perfecte shape is such : as Cupid feares his fall,
And euery wight that hath her sæne, I say ( not one) but all
With one consent they cry : lo here dame Venus ayer,
Not Danae nor shæ dame Lede : was euer halfe so faire.
Though Princes sue for grace: and ech one do thee woo,
Mislyke not this my meane estate : wherwith I can nought doo,
As highest seates wæ sæ : be subiect to most winde,
So base and poore estates we know , be hateful to the minde.
The happy meane is mine : which I do haply holde,
Thy honor is to yæld for loue : and not for heape of golde.
If euer thou hast felte : the bitter panges that stinges
A louers breest:or knowest the cares, that Cupid on vs slinges.
Then pitty my request : and wayle my wofull case,
Whose life to death with hasty whæles : doo tcumble on apace.
Vouchsafe to ease the paine : that loue on mæ doth whelme,
Let not thy frænd to shipwracke go : sith thou doost hold his helme.
Who yældeth all hæ hath : as subiect to thy will,
If thou commaund hæ doth obey, and all thy heastes fulfill.
But if thou call to minde: when I did part thee fro,
What was the cause of my exile : and why I did forgo

The happy life I held, and lost therewith thy sight,
Well mayst thou wayle thy want of troth:true thy great vnright
If thou be found to fayle thy vow that thou hast sworne
Or that one iot of my good will,out of thy minde be worne.
Or if my absence long: to thy disgrace hath wrought mee          (mée.
Or hindering tales of my back freends:vnto such state hath brought
I can and will accurse the cause of my ill spéede :
But well,I hope, my feare is more : then is the thing indéede.
Yet blame mée not though I do stand somewhat in feare
The cause is great of my exile,which hardly I do beare.
Who hath a sternles ship amidst the trustles Seaes,
Full gréedely desires the porte : where hée may ride at ease.
Thy bewty bids mee trust, vnto thy promise past,
My absence longe and not to speake : doth make mee doubt as fast.
For as the sommers sonne,doth make eche thing to spring:
Euen so the frosen winters blast,as deadly doth them wring.
Vnsuer thus I liue in dreade I wot not why
Yet was there neuer day so bright, but there be cloudes in sky.
Who hath of puer Golde,a running streame or flud
And is restraind for comming nigh , this treasure great and good.
Hée must abide a time : till Fortune graunt him grace,
That hee haue power by force to win: his riche desired place.
I neede not thus to do: nor yet so much mistrust,
I know no time can change thy minde : or make thée bée vniust.
No more then water soft, can stir a stedfast rocke:
Or seely flyes vpon their backes can beare away a blocke.
Eche beast on earth wée sée : that liuing breath doth draw,
Bée faythfull found vnto their mates : and keepes of loue the law.
My wretched life to ease : when I do seke to turne,
Thy bewty bright doth kindle mee,in greater flame to burne.
No day, no night, nor time,that geues mee mirth or rest,
Awake, asleape, and at my meales , thou dost torment my brest.
Though weary lothsome lyfe: in care and wo haue clad mee,
Remembrance of thy heauenly face,giues cause again to glad mée.
Thus Ioyfull thoughtes a while,doth lessen much my payne
But after calme and fayer tides,the stormes do come agayne.

By                    And

And I in cares doo flame, to thinke of my exile,  
That I am barred from thy fight : I curse and ban the while.  
Would God I had the craft a Laborinth to frame,  
And also had a Mynotaure : inclofed in thefame:  
And that our enemies all, might therin take fome paine,  
Till Dedales line I did them bringe, to helpe them out againe.  
Then fhould my forowes feace, and drowne my deepe difpaire,  
Then fhould my life be bleft with Ioyes: and raifed aboue the ayre,  
But as the mazed birde, for feare dare fkautly fly,  
When hee hath fcapte the Falcons fote : euen fo I know fhould I  
Scarfe able be to fpeake, or any word to fay,  
Leaft Argus wayting ielous eyes, might haply mée bewray  
But oh Elrifa mine, why doo I ftir fuch war  
Within my felfe to thinke of this: and yet thy loue fo far?  
Why rather fhould not I : giue vp the life I haue  
And yéeld my weary wretched corps : vnto the gaping grau  
If I hopte not that thou with faith didft binde thy life,  
This hand of mine with blody fworde, fhould ftint my cruel ftrife,  
No length of lingring time: no diftance can remoue,  
The fayth that I haue haue vowed to thée : nor alter once my loue.  
Beleeue this to bee true, that ftreames fhall foner turne,  
Or frofen Ice to fier coales, on blafing flame to burne.  
Then I will feke to change: or alter once my minde,  
All plagues I pray may fall on me, if I be found vnkinde.  
Or if I meane to fwarue while I haue liuing breath  
God graunt my end then may be fuch as Agamemnons death.  
I wifh thy life no harme: but yet I woulde thou knew  
The woful! ende that Creffed made, becaufe fhee was vntrue.  
Thofe angry gods or men, afonder that doo fet vs,  
Shal neuer pearce our mindes in twaine nor eke to loue can let vs  
As well they may deuide the fier from the flame,  
And euery beaft that now is wilde, as foone fhalbe made tame.  
Let not this piftle long, my fute with thée deface,  
Who pleadeth for his life thou knoweft: at large muft tel his cafe.  
And all thefe wordes I write, to one effect do tende,  
I am all thine, and not mine owne : and herewithal to ende.

I

## of gallant Inuentions.

I pray thee to regarde: thy health and my requeſt,
And that my loue doo neuer fleet out of thy ſecret breſt.
FINIS.

¶ NARSETVS a wofull youth, in his exile writeth
to Roſana his beloued miſtreſſe, to aſſure her of his
faithfull conſtancie, requiring the like of her.

O ſtay thy muſinge minde : hee did this piſtle frame,
That holds thee deere, & loues thee moſt: Narſetus is his name
Would God thy frend had brought: ý health ý here he ſendes
I ſhould haue ſeene my lacking ioy, and heale that hart that rendes,
And redy is eche hower : to ſunder ſtill in twaine,
Saue now this piſtle that I write : doth leſſen wel my paine,
And helpes mee to vpholde a lingring lothſome life,
Awaiting ſtill the bliſſull hower, when death ſhall ſtinte the ſtrife.
What doeth it mee preuaile : to haue king Creſus wealth,
Or who doth ioy in golden Giues, impriſoned with his health,
I ſweare by loue to thee, whoſe godhead is aye iuſt,
Theſe wordes I write are not vntrue : then do mee not miſt ruſt.
Thy ſelfe ſhalbe the iudge : and if thou liſt to vewe,
The bared bones, the hollow lookes, the pale and ledy hew,
The ſtealing ſtrides I draw : the wo and dreadfull feares
The boyling breſt with bitter brine, the eyes be ſprent with teares
The ſkant and hungry meales : the ſeldome ſlepe I take,
The dainty dames that others ioy, no ieſt to mee do make
Theſe hated hatefull harmes: when I them feele to greeue mee
Remembrance of thy beuty bright, doth ſtraight again releeue mee
And then I cal to minde, thy ſhape and cumly grace,
Thy heauenly hew thy ſugred wordes, thy ſweet entiſing face
The pleaſant paſſed ſportes : that ſpent the day to ende,
The lothſom lookes that liked not to leue ſo ſoone thy freend.
Sith froward fortune hath, my Myſtreſſe thus bereft mee,
Perforce I yeeld and am content, to like the lot is left mee.
If Pyramus were ſad, when hee found Thisby ſlayne,
If Creſſeds craft and falſing fayth : did Troylus turne to payne,

B iij                                              Eneas

Eneas traytoʒ falſe : oh treaſon that hǽ did,        (hath riʒ
With bloody woundes and murdering ſwoʒd, Quǽne Didos lyfe
If theſe haue won by death and end of pyning payne,
And J aliue with toʒments great in dying deathes remaine.
The ſound of inſtruments: oʒ muſickes pleaſant noyce,
Oʒ riches rule, oʒ pʒoude eſtate, doth cauſe mǽ to reioyce
Oʒ Venus damſels deere, do pleaſe mǽ euen as well,
As dying bodies ioy to here, foʒ them a paſſing bell.
The grǽfes that gripe my hart, and dayly do mǽ ſlay
Jt leſſen would much of the ſmart, if thou bouchſafe to ſay:
God graunt his weary life : and ſoʒrowes to aſſwage,
God yǽld him health and happy dayes with honoʒ in his age.
Theſe woʒdes would win my life, diſpaired now to death,
Thou ſhould but ſaue that is thine own, while J haue liuing bʒeath
What heapes of haples hopes, on me ſhall chance to fall,
So thou doo liue in bliſfull ſtate: no foʒce foʒ mǽ at all.
Amid my greateſt grǽfe, the greateſt care J haue,
Js how to wiſh and will thǽ good: and moſt thy honoʒ ſaue.
Bǽ faythfull found therfoʒe, bǽ conſtant true and iuſt
If thou betray thy louing frǽnd, whom henſfoʒth ſhall J truſt?
When ſhal J ſpeake with thee? when ſhal J thee imbʒace? (graceʒ
When will the gods appeaſe their wʒath? when ſhal J haue ſuch
Hath Ioue foʒgotten dame Lede foʒ loue : and how hee pʒayed her,
Transfoʒmed like a ſwan at length: the ſǽly ſoule hee trayde her.
When faire freſh Danae was cloſed vp in tower :
Did hee not raine himſelfe a dʒop, amidſt the golden ſhower
And fell into her lap : from top of chimney hic?
The great delight of his long loue: hee did attaine thereby,
What cruell gods be theſe? what treſpaſſe haue J doone?
That J am baniſht thus from thee, what conqueſt haue they woon?
J know their power deuine : can foʒ a while remoue mee,
But whilſte J liue, and after death, my ſoule ſhall likewiſe loue thǽ
Not Alcumena ſhee, foʒ whom the treble night
Was ſhaped firſt, can well compare with thee foʒ bewty bʒight
Not Troylus ſiſter too, whom cruell Pirrhus ſlew,
Noʒ ſhee, the pʒice of ten yeres wars, whom yet the Greckes do rew
                                             Noʒ

Noz thee Penelope, whofe chaftnes wan her fame,
Can match with thee Rofina chafte: I fee her blufh foz fhame.
The childe of mighty Ioue, that bzed within his bzaine
Shall yeeld the palme of filed fpeche,to thee that doth her ftaine.
And euery wight on earth : that liuing bzeath do dzaw,
Lo here your queene fent from aboue,to kepe you all in awe
But nowe I fine my talke, I finde my wits to dull,
There liueth none that can fet fozth thy vertues at the ful.
Yet this I dare well fay,and dare it to auowe,
The Gods do feare Rofinas fhape: and bewty doth alowe.
In Tantalus toyle I liue : and want that moft I would,
With wifhing vowes I fpeake,I pzay: yet lacke the thing I fhould
I fee that I do want: I reach,it runnes mee fro:
I haue and lacke,that I loue moft, and lotheft to fozgo.
But oh Rofanna dere: fince time of my exile                (while
How haft thou done? and dooft thou liue:how haft thou fpent the
How ftandeth health with thee:and art thou glad of chere?
God graunt thofe happy reftful dayes,increafe may ftill each yere.
If any greefe oz care,do vex thy wofull hart,
Then God I pzay to giue thee eafe,and fwagement of thy fmart.
Yet this I doo defire, that thou be found to abide
A freend: euen fuch as fhal miflike,with fodaine change to flide.
If pleafure now thou haft,to fpend the dzeiry day,
Read then this piftle of my hande,to dziue the time away.
If all thy freendes aliue: would from thy frendfhip fwarue,
A thoufand deathes I do defire,in wzetched ftate to ftarue.
If I amongft the reft,fhould alter fo my minde,
Oz thou fhouldeft charge I pzomife bzake,oz els am found vnkinde
Though Argus iclus eyes: that daily on vs tend,
Fozbid vs meat and fpeech alfo, oz meffage foz to fend.
A time will come to paffe,and thinke it not to long
That thou and I fhall ioyne in ioy, and wzeake vs of our wzong.
Which time I would abide : though time too long doth try mee
In hope againe when time fhal ferue,thou wilt not then deny mee
Thus hope doth mee vpholde: foz hope of after bliffe,
And lofe therby my pzefent ioy,in hoping ftill foz this.

                                                                  I OO

I doo commend to thee : my life and all I haue,
Commaund them both as thee best likes: to lose o₂ els to saue.
I am no mo₂e mine owne, but thine to vse at will
Thesame is thine without desert, if thou mee seke to kill.
Bee glad thou litle quere, my mystresse shall thee see
Fall flat to ground befo₂e her face: and at her feet doo lie :
Haste not to rise againe, no₂ doo her not withstand
If of her bounty shee vouchsafe, to rayse thee with her hand.
Say thy maister sent thee, and humbly fo₂ mee greete her, (her.
Thou knowest my selfe doth wish full ofte: to be in place to meete
If any wo₂de in this, hath scapte and doo her greeue,
A pardon craue vpon thy knee, and p₂ay her to fo₂geue
A giltles hand it w₂ote, thou mayst be bolde to tell:
No minde of malice did mee moue, her self doth know it well.
Thou canst and I deserue : make glad my wofull sp₂ite,
I craue no answer to thy payne : no₂ fo₂ce thee fo₂ to w₂ite.
It should suffise if thou: vouchsafe to reade the same,
This pistle then if thou mislyke, condemne it to the flame.
But now there needes no mo₂e, I will this pistle ende,
Estéeme Narsetus alwayes well: that is thy faythfull frénd,

**FINIS.**

The Louer forsaken, writeth to his Lady
a desperate Farwell.

Hen hée that whilome was: thy faithful frénd most iust,
That th₂ise th₂ée yéeres hath spent & past, reposing all his
In thy bewayling wo₂ds, that sémed sugar swéet (trust
The selfsame man vnwillingly: doth with these lines thée
I can not speake with thee: and speaking is but paine, (gréet.
To speake and p₂ay and not to spéede : too fruitles were the gayne.
Info₂ste therfo₂e I w₂ite, and now vnfolde my minde,
I loue, and like as earst I did, I am not yet declinde.
Though time that trieth all, hath turnde the loue you ought,
No changing time could alter mee: o₂ w₂est awry my thought.

And

# of gallant Inuentions.

And sure I do mislyke, that wemen choose to change,
Ungratefull folkes I do detest, as monsters foule and strange.
Sith first I did you know: I neuer spake the thing
That did intend you to beguile, or might repentance bring.
Thrise hath my pen falne downe: vpon this paper pale,
And scantly can my hart consent: to write to thee this tale.
Least hasty Iudgmentes might, misdeeme my giltles minde,
To charge that malice moues my speech, or some new frend to finde
The gods I vouch to ayd: who knowes the troth I ment,
To swarue or fleet from that I vowed, was neuer my intent.
But as the Courser fearce, by pearcing spur doth run,
So thy desertes enforce mee now: to see this worke begun.
Would God I had no cause to leaue that I did loue,
Or lothe the thing that likt mee so : nor this mishap to proue.
But sith nothing in earth : in one estate can bide,
Why striue I then against the streame, or toyle against the tide?
And haue you now forgot, how many yeeres I sought,
To get your grace with whot good will: how dearly I it bought.
There is no one aliue, that nature euer made
That hath such giftes of vertues race, and such vntroth doth shade.
If fayth might haue bin found, within a womans brest,
I did beleeue within thy hart, shee chose her place to rest.
Unskilful though I bee, and cannot best deserne,
Where craft for troth doth preace in place, yet am I not to learne.
And I did thinke you such: that litle knew of guile,
But seemings now be plaste for deedes, and please fulwel the while
Why doo I wunder thus? to thinke this same so strange,
Who hath assayed and knoweth not? that wemen choose to change.
Haue you thus sone forgot, the doutes and dreades you made,
Of yongmens loue how litle holde, how sone away they fade.
How hardly you beleeued: how often would you say,
My wordes were spoken of the splene : and I as oft denay.
How oft did you protest with handes vpstretcht to skyes?
How oft with othes vnto the Gods? how oft with weeping eyes?
Did you beseech them all, to rid your spending dayes?
When that you thought to leaue your frend: to dy without delayes

C                                         By

Mée thought in heauen I saw: how Ioue did laughe to skozne,
To sée you sweare so solemly, and ment to be fozswozne.
But as the Sirens singe, when treason they procure,
So smyling baytes the harmles soules : vnto their bane alure.
Thy fawning flattering wozdes, which now full false I finde,
Perswades mée to content my selfe, and turne from Cressids kinde.
And all the sozte of those : that vse such craft I wish
A spéedy end, oz lothsome life, to liue with Lasars dish.
Pet pardon I do pzay: and if my wozdes offend,
A crased ship amid the streame, the Marriner must mende.
And I thus to it and turnd: whose life to shipwzacke goes
Complaynes of wzongs thou hast mée don, and all my gréefe fozth
And could your hart consent? and could you grée therto? (showes.
Thus to betray your faythful fréend, and pzomis to vndo?
If nought your wozdes could binde, to holde your suer behest,
Noz ought my loue ne othes you sware, could bide within your bzest
Pet foz the wozldly shame, that by this facte might rise,
Oz foz the losse of your good name, foz dealing in this wise.
Oz thus to sée mée gréeu'd : tozmented still in payne,
Thy gentil hart should haue bin pleasde such murder to refrayne.
But through thy cruell déede: if that vntamed death,
With spéedy dart shall rid my life, oz leaue my lyuing bzeath.
The gods then can and will: requite thy bloddy acte,
And them I pzay with lowly sute, foz to reuenge thy facte.
God graunt the earth may bzing : nought fozth to thy auayle,
Noz any thing thou takest in hand, to purpose may pzeuayle.
Thy most desired fréend, I wish may bée most coy,
Wherin thou dost thée most delite: and takest the greatest ioy.
That same I would might turne : vnto thy most mischéefe,
That in thy life thy hart may féele, the smart of others gréefe.
But sith no good can come: of thy mishap to mée,
I graunt some blame I doo deserue, that thus desire to sée
Thy blissfull life so changde, from weale to wzetched state,
When fréendes do bzeake the bonde of loue, then is their greatest
Thy déedes do sure deserue, much moze reuenging spight, (hate.
Then hart can thinke oz tongue can tel, oz this my pen can wzight.

                                                        Thy

Thy bewty bright is sutch, that well it would inuade,
A hart more hard then Tigar wilde: and more it can perswade.
Then Tullyes cunning tongue: or Ouids louing tale,
Well may I curse and ban them both, that so haue brewed my (bale.
I feare to praise to far : least haply I begin,
To kindle fier that well is quencht, and burne mée all within.
For well I may compare: and boldly dare it say,
Thou art the Quéene of women kinde, and all they ought obay.
And all for shame doo blush, when thou doost come in place,
They curse ech thing that gaue thée life, and more disdain thy face.
Then any liuyng wight: doth hate the Serpent foule,
Or birdes that singe and flies by day, abhors the shrikyng Owle.
Oh that a constant minde: had guided forth thy dayes,
I had not then assayd myshap: nor pen spoke thy dispraise.
Decréed sith that thou art, for euer to forsake mée,
In sorrows swéete I wil mée shrine: till death shall list to take mée,
Bewayle O woful eyes, with fluds of flowing teares,
This great mischaunce thy lothsome life, that all ill hap vp beares,
Since parted is your ioy, resigne likewise your sight,
I neuer will agrée to like, or looke on other wight.
Nor neuer shall my mouth consent to pleasant sound,
But pale and leane with hollow lookes : till death I will bée found.
And you vnhappy handes : with lyking foode that fed mée,
Leaue of to labor more for mée: since sorrow thus hath sped mée.
Lament vnlustie legges: bée lame for euer more,
Sith shée is gone for whom you kept: your willing pace in store.
O hatefull heauy hart : bewayle thy great vnrest,
Consume thy selfe or part in twaine : within my blouddy brest.
And yée my sences all: whose helpe was aye at hand,
To length the life that lingreth now, and lothsomely doth stand.
Yée sonne, ye moone and starres : that gyues the gladsome light
Forbeare to show your force a while: let all bée irkesome night.
Let neuer soyle bringe forth, agayn the lusty gréene
Nor trées that new dispoyled are, with leafe be euer séene.
Let neither birde nor beast: posses their wonted minde
Let all the thinges that liues on earth, be turned from their kinde.

Let all the furies forth, that pine in Hell with payne,
Let all their torments come abroad: with lyuing wightes to rayne.
Let peace be turnd to war, let all consume with fier,
Sith I must dye that once did ioy, and lose that I desier.
I hate my life and breath, I hate delighting food,
I hate my greefe I hate my death : I hate that doth mee good.
I hate the gentill hart: that rueth on my payne.
I hate the cruell stubborn sorte, that doth my life disdayne.
I hate al sortes of men, that haue their life in prize,
And those I hate that folow death, esteeming them vnwise
I hate those carefull thoughtes that thinke on my sweet so,
I hate my selfe then twice as much : if I forget her so.
I hate, what would you more, I wot not what I hate,
I wish her dead and layed in graue: I wish her better state.
Come wilde and sauadge beastes, stretch forth your cruell pawes,
Dismember mee, consume my flesh : imbrew your greedy iawes.
Within your entrayles: see a coffin ye prepare,
To tombe this carefull corpes that now, vnwillingly I bare.
Come lingringe slothful death: that doost the wretch deny
To show thy force and riost the riche, that list not for to dye.
Is this the recompence? is this the due reward?
Doth loue thus pay his seruants hier? and doth hee thus regard?
And doth hee vse to set, the harmles soules on fier,
With faire sweet intisinge lookes : to kindle their desier?
Fye false loue that hast so decte, with bewty bright,
A Lady faire with such vntroth, to worke such cruell spight.
And ye that doo pursue blinde loue with speedy pace,
Restraine your steps example take, of this my wofull case.
Let this alone suffise, that in few wordes I say,
Who can beware by others harmes, thrice blest and happy they.
Beleeue this to bee true: that now to true I proue,
But litle troth in womens breast: and fleeting in their loue.
God graunt each wight on earth, that serues with faythfull minde,
A better hap and that hee may, a truer Mystrisse finde.

## FINIS.

# of gallant Inuentions.

### The Louer in diftreffe exclaymeth agaynft Fortune.

HOw can the criple get, in running race the game?
Oz hee in fight defend himfelfe, whofe armes are bzoken lame?
How can th'impzifoned man whofe legs be wzapt in chaynes,
Thinke this his life a pleafant time, who knoweth nothing but
So how can I reioyfe, that haue no pleafant thing,                (paines?
That may reuiue my doulfull fpzits, oz caufe mee foz to finge.
My legs be lame to goe, mine armes cannot embzace,
My hart is foze, mine eyes bee blinde, foz lacke of Foztunes grace.
All this is Foztunes fault, that keepes thefe fences fo,
Shee may aduaunce them if fhee lift, and rid them of this wo.
It is her cruell will, alwayes on mee to lower,
To kepe frõ mee her pleafant giftes, to make mee know her power.
Alas, alas, fis Fortune, fie: why art thou fo vnkinde,
To mee that fayne would bee thy fonne, and euer in thy minde?
Now do I thee befeech, with pleafures mee to frayght,
To temper this my wofull life, oz els to kill mee frayght.

## FINIS.

### An other complaint on Fortune.

IN doubtful dzeading thoughts, as I gan call to minde,
This wozld, and eke the pleafures al, that Adams childzen
A place of pleafant hew appeared to my thought (finde,
Where I might fee the wonderous wozks which nature
All things of any pzice, appzoched to my fight,          (foz vs wzought.
And ftill me thought that each man had, that was his moft delight.
The riche man hath his ioy: his riches to imbzace,
So hath the huntefman his defire, to haue the Hart in chace.
And other haue their spozte to fee the Falcon flee,
And fome also in Pzinces court : in fauoz foz to bee.
The warring Knight at will, an hozfe doth run his race,
And eke the louer, in his armes, his Lady doth embzace.
                                                    When

# The gorgious Gallery

When that I sée eche man enioy his whole delite,
Saue I alas poore cursed man whom Fortune doth so spite.
I fall straight to the ground, amazed with much griefe,
With bouddy strokes vpon my brest, I striue to rid my lief.
And thus I thinke, how can fayre pictures those delight:
Whom nature from their tender age, defrauded of their sight.

### FINIS.

¶ The louer beeing newly cought in Cupids snares, complayneth
on the Gods of loue, and compareth his greefe as followeth.

The hugie heape of cares, that in this world I finde,
   The sodayne sighes that sore molest my hart
   The foolish fansies that still run in my minde:
    Makes mée to lay all ioy and myrth apart,
Lamenting still the causes of my smart.
  But oh, alas, the more I wéepe and wayle,
  The more my gréefe to mée séemes to preuayle.

The more I seeke my pinchinge panges to swage,
  By diuers wayes, such as I thinke be best
The more it frets, the more it gins to rage,
  So that my senceles head can take no rest:
Ah seely wretch, what doth thee thus mollest
  Or what doth thus perturbe thy restlesse braynes,
  And from thy harte all worldly ioye detaynes.

Alas what this should bee I can not tell,
  My youthfull yeares can skill of no such change
But if some vgly shape of fury fell:
  Or wicked wight that in this world doth range
Hath witched mée with this disease so strange.
  Or Cupid with his force of cruell dart,
  Hath stricken mée and wounded thus my hart.

Hath

Hath Cupid then sutch power on mortall wightes?
And strikes the blinded boy his dart so sure?
That no man can auoyd his subtill slightes,
Nor ought agaynst his fury may indure?
Hath Venus force men thus for to allure?
And why then?doth shee not her sonne commaund
To shoote alike and strike with equall hand?

Is this the guise of powers that raigne aboue,
Us seely soules in snares thus for to trap
And care they not to yeeld vs death for loue?
Ioy they in woes our corses for to trap?
And passe they not what vnto vs doth hap?
Can Gods aboue to man beare any hate,
Or do they mocke and iest at our estate?

Ah foolish foole?what fancy rules thy head,
Or what doth cause thee now this talke to moue?
What fury fell doth thee poore wretch now lead?
To rayle on all the Gods doth it behoue?
Sith it is only Cupid God of loue.
That guiltlesse shee with stroke of goulden shafte,
Hath wounded thus and thee of ioyes berafte.

Euen as the slender Barke that long is tost
By surging waues cast vp from deepest seas:
And Saylars still in daunger to be lost,
Doo hale and pull in hope to take their ease :
When stormy sluds begin once to appease.
Euen so fare I beeing in Cupids power
In hope at last to see that happy hower.

Wherin I shall my wished ioyes obtayne,
And placed bee within her gentill hart,
Then shall I take my sorrowes all for gayne.
When I haue her that causeth now my smart,

C iiij

Then

# The gorgious Gallery

Then farewell Cupid with thy cruell darte
And welcome shee that pearst mæ with her sight,
Shæ is my Ioy, shæ is my hartes delight.

## FINIS.

The Louer extolleth, aswell the rare vertues of his Lady
beloued, as also her incomparable beautie.

Desire hath driuen from mæ my will,
Or Cupids blase hath bleard mine eyes:
Knowledge mæ fayles, my sight is yll:
If kinde or cunning could deuise
Nature to paynt in better plight
To set her forth with red and white:
Or if men had Apelles arte,
Who could her mend in any parte?

Her face declares where fauor growes,
And telles vs heere is Beauties grace:
Her eyes hath power to binde and lose,
Her countenance may frændes embrace.
Her chækes be decte with blond full fayre,
Her collour cleare as is the ayre:
Her haire, her hand, her foote also,
Hath wonne the praise where euer shæ go.

Her lokes do sæme to speake alone,
When that her lips remoue no whit
Her inwarde vertues may be knowen:
By vsinge of her sober wit.
Her iestures also cumly are,
My tongue lackes skill them to declare:
The rest of her that are vnnamed,
In perfect shapes are lyuely framed.

Now

## of gallant Inuentions.

Now though that kinde hath set her forth,
And natures workes shée hath possest,
Théese goodly giftes are litle worth :
If pitty dwelt not in her brest.
Oh, God forbid such flowring youth
Should bée mislyked for lacke of ruth,
For I with other might say then :
Lo, this is shée that killeth men.

### FINIS.

¶ The Louers farewell, at his departure, perswadeth his
beloued to constancie in his absence.

Though Fortune cannot fauor
  According to my will :
The proofe of my behauor :
  Shall bée to loue you still.

Entending not to chaunge,
  Whiles that my life doth last :
But still in loue to raunge :
  Till youth and age be past.

Though I bée far you fro,
  Yet in my fantacie :
I loue you and no mo :
  Thinke this assuredly.

Your owne both true and iuste,
  Alwayes you shall mée finde :
Wherfore of right you must,
  Haue mée likewise in minde.

And do not mée forsake,
  Though I do tarry longe :

But take mée for your make,
  I will not chaunge my songe.

Though absence now a while,
  Do part vs thus in twayne :
Thinke neither craft nor gyle,
  For I will come agayne

The same man that I went.
  Both in my woorde and déede :
Though some men do relent,
  And grudge that I should spéed.

But if you do remayne,
  And do not fro mée starte :
My hart you do attayne,
  Till death vs two depart.

And thus farewell adew,
  And play an honest parte :
And chaunge mée for no new,
  Séeing that you haue my hart.

### FINIS.

D.

# The gorgious Gallery

A propper Dittie.   To the tune of lusty Gallant;

He glyttering showes of Floras dames
  Delightes not so my carefull minde,
Ne gathering of the fragrant flames :
That ofte in Floras Nimphes I finde.
Ne all the noates of Birdes so shryl
Mellodiously in woods that singe,
Whose solemne Quires the skyes doth fill :
  With noate on noate that heauenly-ringe.

The friskinge Fish in streames that springe
  And sporte them on the riuers side,
The Hound the Hauke and euery thinge:
  Wherin my ioyes did once abide,
Doth nothinge els but bræde my wo
  Sith that I want which I desier,
And death is eke become my fo :
  Denying that I most requier,

But if that Fortunes frændly grace
  Would graunt mine eyes to take the vew,
Of her whose porte and amorous face
  My senses all doth so subdew.
That raunging too and fro to gayne
  The pray that most delighteth mæ,
At last I finde that bræedes me payne :
  Shæ flyes so fast it will not bæ.

Then in my selfe with lingering thoughts
  A sodayne strife begins to gro,
I then doo with such Birdes at noughts :
  That from their louers flyeth so.
At last I sæ the Fowlars gin,
  Prepared for this Birde and mæ
Then wisht I lo his hed therin :
  So that my birde and I were frǣ.

### FINIS.

¶ The Louer perſwadeth his beloued, to beware the
deceites and allurements of ſtrange ſuters.

Be ſtedfaſt to thine owne
　As hee is vnto thee,
Regard not men vn knowen
But loue thine owne truly
For oft deceyts are ſowen
By them that vnknowen bee
　Wherfore caſt of the reſt:
　And thine own loue thou be ſt.

For though that their falſe ſuite
Seeme pleaſant in thine eare,
Thou knowſt oft times ill fruit
A pleaſant tree doth beare.
If thou chaunce to repute
A rotten Apple cleare,
　Better to loue thine owne
　And forſake men vnknowne.

Thou doſt well vnderſtand
Theſe wordes not ſpoken ſeilde
More ſuer a birde in hand,
Then twenty in the feild. (band
Thou knoweſt thine owne ſure
And how that it hath helde
　Then chaunge it for no new:
　But loue him that is trew.

If ſuters do thee moue
Or dayly to thee write,
Yet graunt to them no loue
Their paynes for to requite.
But thinke it doth behoue
Thee alwayes to do right
　Thee muſt thou loue thine own
　And forſake men vnknowne.

This counſayle I thee giue
As farforth as I can,
As I that whiles I liue
Wilbee thine onely man.
For ſure it would mee greene,
To ſee thee out of frame
　Or chaunge at any time:
　Thine owne not to bee thine.

Thus written by thine owne
To thee with all his harte,
Deſiringe the vnknowen
Of thee may haue no part.
For if ſutch chaunge bee ſowen
No doubt thou killeſt my hart
　Wherfore I ſay beware:
　Alwayes the vnknown ſnare.

FINIS.

# The gorgious Gallery

¶ The Lady beloued exclaymeth of the great
vntruth of her louer.

Wuld god I had neuer séen,
 the teares of thy false eyne
Or els my eares ful deaf had bin
That herd those wordes of thine

Then should I not haue knowne
 Nor chosen to my part:
So many euils in one
 To kill my poore true hart.

As now in thée I finde,
 Who bidst mée from thée go :
As false and full vnkinde,
 Alas why doost thou so ?

Was neuer man so false of othe,
 To none as thou to mee
Was neuer womã of more troth
 Then I haue ben to thee.

And thou to leaue mee so,
 And canst no iust cause tell :
But wilt thou spill with wo,
 The hart that loues thee wel.

Hée thinkest that for my part,
 I may speake in the same,
I say me thinkes thou art,
 Euen very much to blame.

Pardy, it is but litle praise,
 To thée that art a man :

To finde so many crafty wayes,
 To frande a poore woman.

At whom all women smile ,
 To sée so fonde on thee :
And men although they wayle,
 To sée how thou blest mee.

To lure mee to thy fist,
 To ease thy feigned payne :
And euer when thou list ,
 To cast mee of agayne.

     (his dayes,
The wretched hound ý spendes
 And serueth after kinde :
The Horse that tredeth ý beaten
 As nature doth him binde (wayes.

In age yet findes releefe,
 Of them that did him wo :
Who in their great mischeefe,
 Disdayne not them to know.

Thus they for wo and smart,
 Had ease vnto their paine :
But I for my true hart,
 Get nought but greefe agayne.

The weary and long night
 doth make mee dreame of thee,
And still me thinks with sight,
 I sée thee here with mee.

       And

And then with open armes,
  I strayne my pillow softe :
And as I close mine armes,
  mee thinkes I kisse thee ofte.

But when at last I wake
And finde mee mockte w dremes
Alas, with mone I make
  My teares run down like strea-
                         (mes.
All they that here this same,
  Wyll spit at thy false deede:

And bid, fie on thy cursed name,
  And on thy false seede.

That shewest so to the eye,
  And bearest so false an hew :
And makest all women cry,
  Lo, how ye men be vntrew?

But yet to excuse thee now,
  To them that would thee spot:
Ile say, it was not thou,
  It was mine owne poore lot.

## FINIS.

¶ The Louer declareth his paynfull plight
       for his beloued sake,

Since needes ye will mee singe, giue eare vnto the voyce,
Of mee poore man your bond seruant, y knoweth not to re-
Consider wel my care, my paine and my vnrest: (ioyce.
Which thou with force of Cupids Dart hast grafted in my
Heale, and withdraw from mee, the venim of that Darte (brest.
Haue pitty, and release this wo, that doth consume my hart :
The greatnes of my greefe, doth bid mee seeke release
I seeke to finde to ease my payne, yet doth my care encrease.

I cease not to beholde, that doth augment my payne :
I see my selfe I seeke my wo, yet can I not refrayne,
That should my wo release, doth most encrease thesame,
The colde that should acquench the heat, doth most enrage the flame
My pleasure is my payne, my game is most my greefe
My cheefe delite doth worke my wo, my hart is my releefe
Sutch haps doth hap to them, that happeth so to loue,
And hap most harde : so fast to binde, that nothing can remooue.

D·iij                    Lo2

# The gorgious Gallery

For when the harme is fired, and rooted in the hart,
No tongue can tell, nor pen may write, how greuous is the smart
I haue thought loue but play, vntill I felte the sore,
But now I felte a thousand greefes I neuer felt before.
To tell what paynes I hide, if that I could deuise,
I tel the truth, beleeue mee wel, the day will not suffise
Graunt now therfore some rest, since thus thou hast mee bound,
To be thine owne, til body mine, lye buried vnder ground.

### FINIS.

¶ The Louer hauing his beloued in suspition
declareth his doutfull minde.

Deeme as ye list vpon good cause
   Yee may, and thinke of this or that,
But what, or why, my selfe best knowes,
   Wherby I thinke and feare not.
Wherunto I may wel like
   The doubtful sentence of this clause
I would ye were not as I thinke
   I would I thought it were not so.

If that I thought it were not so,
   Though it were so, it greeued mee not,
Vnto my hart it were as tho
   I harkened and I heare not.
At that I see I cannot winke,
   Nor for my hart to let it go
I would it were not as I thinke
   I would I thought it were not so.

Lo how my thought might make mee free,
   Of that perchance it needeth not
For though no doubt in deede I see,
   I thinke at that I beare not,

Yet

Yet in my hart this worde shall sinke,
Untill the proofe may better bée
I would it were not as I thinke,
I would I thought it were not.

### FINIS.

¶ An excellent Sonet, wherin the Louer exclaymeth agaynst
Detraction, beeing the principall cause of all his care.
To the tune, when Cupid scaled first the Fort.

PAsse forth in doulfull dumpes my verse,
Thy Masters heauy haps vnfolde :
His grisled grœfe cache hart well perce,
Display his woes, feare not, bée bould
Hid hole in heapes of heauinesse
His dismale dayes are almost spent,
For fate, which forgde this sicklenesse
My youthly yeares with teares hath sprent.

I lothe the lingring life I led
O wished death why stayest thy hand,
Sith gladsome Ioyes away bée fled :
And linkte I am in Dollors bande.

In weltring waues my ship is tost
My shattering sayles away bée shorne,
My Anker from the Stearne is lost
And Tacklings from the Maynyard storne.

Thus driuen with euery gale of winde
My weather beaten Barke doth sayle,
Still hoping harbor once to finde
Which may these passinge perrils quayle.

But out alas, in vayne I hope
Sith Billowes prowd, assault mée still
And skill doth want with Seas to cope
And licour salte my Bale doth fill.

D.iiij.

Yet ſtorme doth ceaſe: but lo at hand
A ſhip with warlike wightes addreſt,
Which ſeemes to bee ſome Pyrates band:
With Powder and with Pellets preſt.

To ſinke or ſpoyle my bruſed Barke
Which dangers dread could not a daunt,
And now the ſhot the ayre doth darke:
And Captayne on the Deke him daunt.

Then Ignorance the overſeear proude
Cryes to Suſpicion, ſpare no ſhot:
And Envy yelleth out aloude,
Yeeld to Detraction this thy Boate:

And as it is now Sea mens trade
When might to coole the foe doth lacke,
By bayling foretop ſigne I made
That to their lee I mee did take.

Then gathering winde to mee they make,
And Treaſon firſt on borde doth come
Then followes Fraud like wily Snake:
And ſwift amongſt them takes his rome.

Theſe binds mee Captiue, tane with band
Of carkinge care and fell annoy,
While vnder Hatches yet I ſtand
Therby quight to abandon ioye.

Then hoyſting ſayles they homeward hye
And mee preſent vnto Diſdayne,
Who mee beheld with ſcorning eye
The more for to encreaſe my payne.

As Lady ſhee commaunded ſtrayght
That to Diſpayre they mee conuay,
And bid with ſkilfull heed bee wayght,
That Truth bee bard from mee away.

Madam (quoth I) let due deſart
Yet finde remorſe for theſe my woes,
Of pitty graunt ſome eaſe to ſmart
Let Troth draw neare to quayle my foes.

But

But all foz nought J dœ complayne
Foz why the deafe can mone no noyse,
No moze can they which dœ disdayne :
But will in harte therat reioyce.

Wherfoze twixt life and death J stay
Til time with daughter his dzawe nye
Which may these furious foes dismay :
Oz els in ruthfull plight J dye.

## FINIS

¶ The Louer in bondage looketh for releasement and
longeth for the releefe of his wedding day.

When shall reliefe release my wo ?
When shall desert,disdayne digest ?
When shall my hap, hap to mœ so ?
That my pooze hart may come tœ rest.
When shall it so ? when shall it so ?

When shall longe loue bœ lœked vpon?
When shall tried truth bœ homeliest?
When shall hope haue that hope hangeth on ?
That my pooze hart may come to rest.
When shall it so ? &c.

When shall J sœ thœ sœethe right ?
When shall J heare shœ heareth mœ best ?
When shall J fœle,shœ fœleth delight ?
That my pooze harte may come to rest.
When shall it so. &c.

When stinte all stozmes that thus agrœue ?
When stinte all stayes that wzong hath wzest ?
When stinte all strifes right to relœue?
That my pooze hart may come to rest.
When shall it so ? &c.

C                                   When

# The gorgious Gallery

When right shall see right time to boste?
When right shall aright vnright oppresse?
When right shall raigne and rule the roste?
Then my poore harte shall come to rest.
    Then shall it so.  &c.
When shall I watch the time to see?
Now shall I wish the time possest,
Now shall I thinke each day yeeres three
That my poore harte may come to rest.
    When shall it so?  &c.
Now farewell harte, most smooth most smart,
Now farewell hart with hart hartiest,
And farewell harte, till hart in harte:
By harty harte may come to rest.
    God graunt it so.  &c.

## FINIS.

¶ A fine and freendly Letter, of the Louer to his beloued.

Like as the Hauke is led by lure, to draw from tree to tree,
  So is my hart through force of loue, where euer my body bee
The Hauke so pray doth double wing, her flight is fled in vayne
I make my flight in waste of winde, my hope receyueth no gayne.
Haukes that be high it hurtes to light, two flightes without reward
My flight is two, and three againe, alas Mistresse regarde: (foode
The Hauke brought low, is soone made high, by feeding on warme
Your mouthes breath settes mee aloft, there is nothing so good.
God Lady then strain forth ye strings, whose tune may mee reuiue
And with straüg tengue do not prolong, my ioyes thus to depriue.
Within your brest my hart is hid, your will and it is one,
Regard my smart, the cure is yours, and losse, when I am gone.
Thus all your owne, I recommend mee wholly to your grace,
As seemeth you best for to reward, my plight and wofull case.
Which plight if you do counterpaise, with ioyes, as doth belonge,
My hart for ioy would tune accorde, to singe some pleasant songe.

## FINIS.

¶ The Louers fata farewell at his death.

AL wealth I must forsake, and pleasures eke forgo,
My life to ende in wo and grǽfe, my desteny is so
For where I had perfixt, with sute to win my ioy,
I found I had right spǽdy death, al welth for to distroy.
Whose Image lo I am, though lyuing I appeare,
Both body and soule be seperate, my heauen it is not here.
My harte I haue bestowed, wheras it is not found
Thou body thē depart thou hence, why pleasurest thou the grounde
And Death draw thou mǽ neare, O Death my dearest frǽnd,
Then with thy dart, shoot through my hart, my sorrows so to ende.
And when that death did heare the thing that I did craue,
Hǽ weighed mǽ, euen as I was, a man fit for the graue.
Come foliow mǽ sayth hǽ, thou man bǽ not agast,
Hǽ that delighteth in earthly thinge, shal fǽle these panges at last
All yǽ then that list to loue, this lesson learne by mǽ,
Or yǽ begin, noate well, the ende, is payne and misery.

### FINIS.

¶ The Louer complayneth of his Ladies vnconstancy
to the Tune of I lothe that I did loue.

You graues of grisly ghosts
　Your charge frō coffins send
Frō roring rout in Plutoes costs
　You Furies vp ascend.

I hate this lothsome life
O Atropos draw nie,
Untwist ȳ thred of mortall strife
　Send death and let mǽ die.

You trampling steades of Hell
　Come teare a wofull wight,
Whose haples hap no tonge can
　Ne pen can well endight. (tell

For Beauties taynted trope
　Hath made my cares assay,
And ficklenes with her did cope:
　To fordge my whole decaye.

　　　　　　　　　　　　E ij　　　　　Ye

My fayth alas I gaue
　To wight of Cressids kinde,
For stedfast loue I loue did craue
As curtesy doth binde.

Shee likewise troth doth plight
　To bee a constant loue,
And proue her self euen maugre
A faythfull turtle Doue. (spight

But lo a womans minde
　Cloakt hole with deepe deceyt
And driuen with euery gale of
To bite at fresher bayt (winde.

For when bewitch shee had
　My minde that erst was free,
And that her cumly beauty bad
My wounded hart agree.

And fixt on Fancyes loue
　As world can witnesse beare,
No other saynct I did adore:
Or Idole any whear

Ne will, no wo, or smart
　Could minde from purpose set,
But that I had a Iasons harte
The golden fleese to get.

Ne for my part I swere
　By all the Gods aboue,
I neuer thought on other fere
Or sought for other loue.

In her the like consente
　I saw ful oft appear,
If eyes be iudge of that it mente
Or eares haue power to heare.

Yet woordes bee turnd to winde
　A new found gest hath got
The Fort, which once, to vnder
And win I planted shot (mine

Her freend that ment her well
　Out of concept is quite,
While other beares away ye bell
By hitting of the white.

In this our wauering age
　So light are womens mindes,
As Aspen leafe ye stil doth rage
Though æole calme his windes.

No place hath due desart
　No place hath constancy (start
In eueri mod their mindes back
As dayly woe may see.

What paps did giue them fod
　That weue sutch webs of wo
What beast is of so cruell mod
That countes his freend for fo:

Yet women doo reward
　With cares the louing wight
They constancy no whit regard,
In change is their delight.

You

# of gallant Inuentions.

You gallant youths therfoze
  In time beware by mee
    FINIS.

Take heed of womes subtil loze,
  Let mee example bee.

¶ The Louer, hauing suftayned ouermuch wrong at his
Ladyes hande wisheth fpeedy death.

TO feeble is the thzead
  That holdeth mee in lyfe,
That if it bee not fuccoured
Shozt end fhal ftint the ftryfe.

Foz though the fpindle ronne
  To dzaw the thzead on length
Alas therby what hold is wonne
If it be weake of ftrength

Oz how can it haue ayde
  Since rigoz is fo rife, (thzead
In her whofe handes to cut the
  Gaue cruelly the knife.

Whofe edge of Enuy hard
  In Venus fozge hath wzought,
Wherby his deth is thus pzeferd
  Whofe life offended nought.

But fithe thy cheefe delite,
  My cheefe delightfull fo, (fpite
Is with fuch wzong to wozk the
  With fpeed come end this wo.

And when my death hath done
  My duty at her will,

A greater greefe be not begonne
  To laft therafter ftill.

Foz after death, if ftrife
  Should ftill my life purfue,
What the doth death but bzeed a
  Of mone & mifcheefe new? (life

Wherfoze if needes thou wilte
  Thy fpindle fpin no moze,
But y this thzed with fpoyle bee
  Which led my life befoze. (fpilt

Pzouide then foz the nonce
  Pzouide foz mee the beft,
That I may dye at once
  From all thy mindes vnreft.

And let not pzefente death
  Pzefer an after paine,
But let the paines pas with my
  And not reuiue againe. (bzeath

Foz thus by this you fhall
  Two thinges at once fulfill,
I fhalbe free that haue bin thzall:
  And you fhall haue your will.

FINIS.

# The gorgious Gallery

¶ The Louer exhorteth his Lady to bee
conſtant.   To the Tune of
Attend thee go play thee.

Of light of loue lady,
Though fancy doo prick thée,
Let conſtancy poſſeſſe thy hart :
Well worthy of blamyng :
They bee, and defaming,
From plighted troth which backe do ſtart:
  Deare dame :
Then ſickleneſſe banniſh,
And folly extinguiſh,
Bee ſkilfull in guiding,
  And ſtay thee from ſlidinge
  And ſtay thee. &c.


The conſtant are prayſed
Their fame high is rayſed
Their worthyneſſe doth pearce the ſkye,
The ſickle are blamed :
Their lightiloue ſhamed,
Theyr fooliſhneſſe doth make them dye :
  As well,
Can Creſſid beare witneſſe,
Fordge of her owne diſtreſſe,
Whom Leproſy paynted
  And penury taynted:
  And penury. &c.


Still Muſes are buſie
To tell vs of Thisbe
Whom ſtedfaſtneſſe doth much commend
And Camma is placed,
To blame the defaced
That light of loue doo ſends.

                  Phedra

Phedra,
Is checked most duly
Because that vntruly
Forst therto by loue light
　Shee slayeth Hippolite.
　Shee slayeth. &c.


A spring of annoyance,
And well of disturbance,
New fanglenesse in loue hath bin:
It killeth the Master,
It poysons the taster,
No worldly wight by it doth win.
　Therfore,
God lady bee constant,
So shall you not bee shent,
But woorthely praysed,
　As you haue deserued,
　As you haue, &c.

### FINIS.

The Louer wounded with his Ladies beauty
craueth mercy. To the Tune of
where is the life that late I led.

F pitty once may moue thy hart,
　To rew a wofull wight?
If curtesy can force thy minde.
　To vew my doulfull plight?
Sith I cannot deuise
　To quench this raging fier,
With tribling teares I craue of thee
　Attend to my desier:
Whom Venus fethered boy
　Hath craide with deadly dart,

　　　　　　　　　　　Sent

Sent from the rayes of those thy eyes
  Which bread my wo and smart.

In vewing thee I tooke sutch ioy
  As wofull wight in rest
Untill the blinded boy I felte
  Assault my captiue brest.
And since that time alas
  Such pinching payne I tasts
That I am now remedilesse
  If mercy make not haste.
For hid in deepe dispayre
  My teares are all my ioy,
I burne, I freese, I sinke, I swim
  My wealth is mine annoy.

Lyke as the tender turtle Doue
  Doth wayle the losse of mate,
In mourning wæd, so spend I tyme
  Lamentinge mine estate.
The night renewes my cares
  When weary limmes would rest,
And dreadfull dreames abandon slepe
  Which bad my græfes represt.
I drench my couch with teares
  Which flow from gushing eyes,
A thousand heapes of hidden thoughtes
  In minde I do deuise.

Full often times it doth mee good
  To haunt and vew the place,
Where I receiued my wound, alas
  By vewing of thy face.
Full oft it ioyes my hart
  To kisse that clot of clay,

From whence thou ſhot thoſe louing lookes
  Which bꝛed my whole decay.
O bleſſed place I cry
  Though woꝛker of my payne,
Render I craue moſt hartely
  To mæ my loue agayne.

Not wofull Monſier dom Dieg
  Oꝛ Priams noble ſonne,
Conſtrayned by loue did euer mone
  As I foꝛ thæ haue donne.
Sir Romeus annoy
  But trifle ſæmes to mine,
Whoſe hap in winning of his loue
  Did clue of cares vntwine.
My ſoꝛrowes haue no ende
  My hap no ioy can ſpie,
The flowing Fountayne of my teares
  Beginneth to waxe dꝛie.

Let pitty then requyte my payne
  O woꝛker of my woe,
Let mercy milde poſſeſſe thy harte
  Which art my fræudly foe.
Receiue the hart which heare
  I yæld into her hand,
Which made by foꝛce a bꝛeach in Foꝛt
  Which I could not withſtande.
Thou haſt in Ballance payſd
  My life and eke my death,
Thy loyalty contaynes my ioy
  Diſdayne will ſtop my bꝛeath.

If conſtant loue may reape his hire
  And fayth may haue his due,

          F                 God

Good hope I haue your gentill hart
   My grislie græfe will rue.
And that at length I shall
   My hartes delight imbrace:
When due desart by curtesse,
   Shall purchace mee thy grace.
Untill which time, my deare
   Shail still increase my payne,
In pensiue thoughtes and heauinesse.
   Because I shall remayne.

## FINIS.

¶ A Caueat to yongmen to shun the snares
of Cupids crafty sleightes.

F euer wight had cause to mone
   or wayle with bitter teares,
His wretched life and wofull plight
   that still in languish weares.
Then haue I cause that late haue lodgde.
   such loue within my hart,
With græfe, with payne, with pyning panges
   my body boyles in smart.

O earth why dost not thou
   my wofull plight sustayne?
O surging Seas with swallowing gulfe
   release mæ of this payne.
For languishing loue with dolefull dœmes
   hath layd my hart in brine,
O wofull wretch, O wicked wight
   That so for loue doth pine.

The Sonne that shines with golden beames
   and dries the dewie flowers,
                    Doth

Doth cause mée wretch with blubbering eyes
    to gush forth extreame showers.
The hermony of chirping birdes
    that ioyes with siluer songes,
Eche lyuing wight, doth cause my cares
    to fill my hart with thronges.

Eche gladsome ioy of mundaine glée
    That glads the worldly minde,
Doth heape vp cares on carefull corps
    agaynst all course of kinde.
And so eche thing that ought delight
    and rid the minde from pause,
Contrariwise agaynst all right
    a thousand cares doth cause.

For when that I in sugred sleepe,
    most swéetly should take rest,
Then do I wring my wofull handes
    and beate my dolefull brest.
And if I chaunce on sleepe to fall,
    a thousand dreames I haue :
And do suppose I her embrace,
    whose want will cause my graue.

And then with gladsome hart I ioy
    thus cleane depriued of wo :
But (oh alas) when that I wake,
    I finde it nothing so.
And then my sighes from sobbing harte
    doth reaue my brest in twayne,
And teares that run from blubbered eyes
    doth more encrease my payne.

And when I should sustayne my lyfe
    and féeble corps with fode,
          F ij            Vnsauory

# The gorgious Gallery

Unsauory séemes it vnto m ée :
  eache thing should doo mee good

Amidst the nipping frostes I broyle,
  in pearching heate I fréese
And thus agaynst all course of kinde :
  for loue my life I léese.
Wo woorth the time that first I lodgde
  thy spoyling loue in harte,
You yonge men al bée warnd by mée
  And shun blinde Cupids Darte

## FINIS.

¶ The aged Louers noate, at length to learne to dye.

Why askest thou the cause
  Wherfore I am so sad
Thou knowst whé age on draws
  No creature can bée glad.

And sith shée hath mée rested
  And threatned mæ to die:
Therfore I am sequestred
  All mirth for to denie.

And now with féeble age
  The rest of all my dayes,
My coütenance must be ful sage:
  Since that my life decayes.

Like as the harte of Oke
  By time doth rot at last,
Like time doth age produce
  With time my hart doth brast.

Lo thus by course of time
  My youth is gone and past,
And now the turne is mine
  Of bitter death to taste.

And noate that I haue sayd
  The cause wherof and why,
My youthfull partes be playde
  And I must learne to die.
## FINIS.

¶ The desperate Louer exclaymeth his Ladyes cruelty
and threatneth to kill himselfe.

My ioyful dayes bée paſt,
  My plaſant yeres be gone,
My life it may not laſt
  My graue and I am one.

My mirth, and all is fled
  And I a man in woo,
Deſireth to bée dead
  My miſchaſe to foꝛgoe.

I burne and am a colde
  I fréeſe in middeſt of fire,
I ſée ſhée dooth with hold
  That moſt I dow deſire.

I ſée that ſhée doth ſée
  And yet ſhée wilbe blinde,
I ſée in healpinge mée
  Shée ſéeketh and wil not finde.

I ſée how ſhée doth wꝛye
  When I begin to mone,
I ſée when I come nye
  How fayn ſhée would be gone.

I ſee ſhee knoweth my harte
  And how I dow complayne,
I ſee ſha knoweth my ſmarts
  Shée ſeeth I dow not fayne.

I ſee my helpe at hand
  I ſee my death alſo.
I ſee where ſhee doth ſtand
  I ſee my cruell fo.

I ſee, what would you moꝛe?
  Shée would mee gladly kill,
And ſhee ſhall ſee therfoꝛe
  That ſhee ſhall haue her will.

I cannot liue by ſtones
  It is to harde a food,
I would be dead at once
  to dow my Lady good.

Shee ſhall haue her requeſt
  And I will haue mine ende,
Lo heere my bloudoy bꝛeſt
  To pleaſe her moſt vnkinde.
    FINIS.

¶ The Louer beeing blinded with the faythleſſe loue of his Lady
is contented to remit her fault vpon promis of amendment.

Since that thou diddeſt mee loue
  When luſt did thee pꝛouoke,
And that thou dooſt well pꝛoue:
  That I cannot reuoke.

My frændſhip faſt, my loue noʒ my good will,
Shew ſome relæfe, leaſt in diſpayʒe I ſpill.


How well I was content
Alwayes to follow thée?
How well I did aſſent,
Thy thʒall aye foʒ to bee
Thy ſelfe can iudge to whom I doo appeale,
By ſentence lo, to yæld mee woo oʒ weale.


But if thou mée foʒſake,
As Creſſid that foʒgot,
True Troylus her make,
And that thy hart is whot                        (die,
On him whom ſhame did foʒce thée once his fayth to
I ſæ no hope but ỹ hæ muſt yæld foʒth himſelf to die.


And though thou thinke that I,
Am loth thee too foʒgoe,
Yet ſhall I rather die
Then liue and pleaſe my foe:
But hindʒe him in loue, all others doth refrayne,
Whoſe treaſõ once did mæ purchace thy due diſdain


### FINIS.


¶ A worthy compariſon of Vertue agaynſt
all worldly pompe.


When that I way with wit, and eke conſider now,
The tickle ſtay of her, that Foʒtunes whæle doth bow
And turne euen at her will, ſuch luck, loe, as ſhee liſt,
No thʒead ſo ſurely ſponne, but that ſhee may vntwiſt.
I can but aye lament, and wayle the lacke of them,
That in her holde doo truſt, weighing they are but men.

For if I were a Lorde, and come of high degree,
And had all thing at will, as best contented mee:
My Prince therwith well pleased, that nothing might offend,
And all my deedes so done, that eche man might commend.
My parent of great state, and eke of worthy fame,
That worldly men did wish, the honor of his name:
My friends and mine allyes so worthy in eche presse,
That I neede beare no wrong, that I could not redresse.
Of courage and of strength, so doughty of my hand,
That Ladyes might mee loue, that dwell in forrayn land,
And enemyes might mee dread, for feare of ouerthrow,
And that all this were true, eche worldly wight did knew,
Yet were I but a man, and mortall in this earth,
For death doth not accept, the worship of my byrth:
Since so I holde it best, that eche man should contend,
So to directe himselfe, that after this liues ende,
Yet vertue might remayne, that soundes a Trompet, loe,
A comfort to a freend, a wound vnto a foe.

*As some to simple turne from sage,*
*And ouerthrow with euery winde,*
*some eke correct with rigorous rage*
*Whom wealth could neuer foord good minde,*
*Hath wonne in prison such a feelde,*
*As liberty could neuer yeelde.*

FINIS.          *Virtute nulla possessio maior.*

¶ Of a happy wished time.

EChe thing must haue a time, and tyme doth try mens troth,
And troth deserues a special trust, on trust great frenship groth:
And freendship is full fast, where faythfulnesse is found
And faythfull thinges be ful of fruicte, and fruitful things be sound
The sound is good in proofe, and proofe is Prince of prayse,
And worthy prayse is such a pearle, as lightly not decayes,

All

# The gorgious Gallery

All this doth time bring forth, which time I must abide,
How should I boldely credit craue? till time my truth haue tried.
And as a time I found, to fall in Fancies frame,
So do I wish an happy time, at large to shew the same.
If Fortune aunswer hope, and hope may haue her hire,
Then shall my hart possesse in peace, the time that I desire.

FINIS.

¶ The Louer perswadeth him selfe to pacience
agaynst Enuie and slanderous tongues.

If only sight suffise, my hart to loose or binde,
  What cause haue I to moue debate, wherby no peace I finde?
If that my restlesse will, by payne doth still renue,
What force haue I:but shee consent, my so for to subdue?
To yeeld and suffer then, I thinke it for the best,
And by desert as time shall serue, to purchase quiet rest.
Let ielous enuy lowre with browes, and visage bent,
I know the worst, no shameles tongue, shall alter myne intent.
The Dice of Loue are throwen, god speede the doubtfull chaunce
Misdeeme who lyst, so shee at last, my seruice will aduaunce.
To aske and to obtayne, that Fortune were so swifte,
Sith trauaill is the ready way, vnto eche noble gyfte.
And feeble is the ioy, that lightly is begonne,
As tender Flaxe can beare no stresse, before that it bee sponne.
Wherfore with sad aduice, in hope my harte shall dwell,
And all the tale that I confesse, in silence will I tell
Vnto her selfe alone, whose fauour I require,
None els shall know her name for mee, to constre my desire.

FINIS.

The

¶ The Louer greeuously complayneth agaynſt the vniuſt
dealing of his Lady beloued.

SInce thou vniuſt, haſt caught a luſt,
　To plough in barrayne ground :
Who long thée loue, hée ſhall thee pzoue,
　Mutch better loſt then found.

As bzickle clay, in Winters day,
　That in the froſt is wzought,
So dœ I finde, thy double minde,
　Mutch better ſolde then bought.

It is as éeſe, a bzoken Syue,
　Should holde the dzopping rayne :
As foz to binde, thy chaunged minde,
　That nought can dœ but fayne.

So may I ſay, both night and day,
　Curſing the time and place:
Where I pzofeſt, to loue thee beſt,
　Whoſe troth I finde ſo ſcace.

Whoſe lyinge wozdes, and faigned bourdes,
　Did mee ſo far enchayne:
When thou didſt flyt, by chaunged wit,
　That I could not refraine.

But of my hart, to eaſe the ſmart,
　The beſt redzeſſe I know:
Is to vntwinde, my conſtant minde,
　And let ſutch fanſies goe.

Foz thoughe I ſerue, vntill I ſterue,
　I ſée none other bœte
　　　　　G　　　　　　　Such

# The gorgious Gallery

Such doublenesse , thy hart doth presse,
   And croppes it by the roote.

Yet will I pray, euen as I may,
   That Cupid will requite,
Thy froward harte, with such a smart,
   As I haue by thy spite.

For to bée fed, with wake a bed,
   And fast at boorde among :
Till thou confesse, ah pittilesse,
   That thou hast doone mée wrong.

On bush and brier , may it appeare,
   Wherby most men doo pas,
Thy faygned fayth, how nere my death,
   It hath mée brought alas.

That they vncaught, may once bée taught,
   By reason to refrayne :
Their crafty wiles, and subtill smiles :
   That so in loue can fayne.

A due vniust, sith that I must,
   Of force declare thée so,
The fault is thine, the payne is mine :
   And thus I let thée go.
        FINIS.

¶ The Louer in great distresse comforteth
      himselfe with hope.

 Heauy hart whose harmes be hid,
   Thy healpe is hurte, thy hap is hard,
If thou shouldest brast, as God forbid :
   Then should I dye without reward.

Hops

Hope well to haue, hate not sweet thought,
Ofte cruell stormes faire calmes haue brought:
After sharp showres, the sunne shyneth fair e,
Hope comneth likewise after dispayre.

In hope a kinge doth go to warre,
In hope the Louer lyues full longe,
In hope the Marchaunt sayles full farre,
In hope most men doo suffer wronge:
In hope the Ploughman soweth much seede,
Thus hope helpes thousands in their neede.
Then faynt not hart amonge the rest,
What euer chaunce hope thou the best.

Though wit biddes will to blowe retrayte,
Wyll cannot worke as wit would wish
When that the Roche doth taste the bayte :
To late to warne the hungry fishe.
When Cities bren of firy flame,
Great Ryuers scarce will quenche the same.
If Will and Fantasie bee agreed
To late for Wyt to bid take heede.

## FINIS.

¶ In the commendacion of faythfull loue.

THe faithful cannot flye, nor wander to nor fro,
Fayth only they holde them bye, though that the fickle go.
A Piller of more force, then Marble layd with hand,
With Pickaxe may deuorce, and lay it flat on land.
Th'other so deuine, that no arte can remoue,
Once layd cannot decline, th'only Piller loue,

## FINIS.

# The gorgious Gallery

¶ The Louer wisheth himselfe an Harte in the Foreste, (as
Acteon was)for his Ladyes sake.

Would I were Acteon, whom Diana did disguise,
To walke the woods vnknown, wheras my lady lies:
A hart of pleasant hew, I wish that I were so,
So that my Lady knew, alone mee, and no mo.

To follow thicke and plaine, by hill and dale alow,
To drinke the water fayne, and feede mee with the sloe:
I would not feare the frost, to lye vpon the ground,
Delight should quite the cost, what payne so that I found.

The shaling nuts and mast, that falleth from the tree,
Should serue for my repast, might I my Lady see:
Sometime that I might say, when I saw her alone,
Beholde thy slaue alone, that walkes these woods vnknowen.

### FINIS.

¶ An Epytaph vpon the death of Arthur
Fletchar of Bangor Gent.

Ye grisly ghostes which walke below in black Cocistus Lakes,
    Mids Ditis dennes, Erebus Dames, with heare of vgly Snakes
Medusa with thy monstrous mates, assist mee now a while,
In dyre wamenting verse to shew, and dzierie dolefull stile.
The fayre vntimely fatall ende of Fletcher, now by death,
Vnto the Ayre his soule with Ioue, resignde his latest breath:
Whose life full due wee must commend, as it deserues the same,
And conuersation to eche one, did seldome meryt blame.
A faythfull freend to eche hee was, to none an oppen foe,
Vnto his Prince a subiect true, till fates had lodgd him loe.
His actes did tend to no mans harmes, no Parasite to prayse,
For greedy gayne but still the troth, mayntaygnd at all assayes.

His

His time hée spent in Uertues loze, as séemd his state full wel,
By serious study what hée could, hée sought foz to excel.
But what of al this same? the fates no wight in time wyll spare,
Whē gastly death hath pearst in earth, thē must our bodyes weare
In age aswell in youthes, in youthes aswell in age,
Ho certayne time wée haue to bide, when death with vs wil wage.
Ho thing can still abide, but comes to nought in ende,
The craggy Rocks the sturdiest okes: starke rotten once is rend.
And so hath Fletcher, now to death payd his due,
What hée is now wée must bée all, his Funerall then vew.

## FINIS.

¶ A Lady writeth vnto her Louer wherin shee most
earnestly chargeth him with Ingratitude.

 Wzetched wight whom hensfoozth may I trust
All men both falce and fell I will them painte,
If thou (vnkinde) bée cruell and vniust
Whom I alwayes so faythfull held and quainte:
What cruelty? what trustles treasons iust?
Was euer hard by tragicall complaint?
But lesse then this, my merit if I may,
And thy desart in equall ballance lay.

Wherfoze (vnkinde) since that on liue?
A wozthier wight cf pzowes ne beauty,
He that by much to thée that doth ariue,
In cumly pozte ne genozositie.
Why dost thou not twéene these thy vertues striue,
It may bée sayd thou hast serbillitie:
Then say that who of fayth is holden stable:
There may to him none els bée comparable.

F iii                                          Fo3

# The gorgious Gallery

For write ye not that vertues haue no grace
Wheras this trust and stablenesse doth want,
As other things, though much of cumly face :
Cannot be seene, where gladsome light is skant.
A mayd to false for thee, an easie case,
Whose Idol, Lord & God thou werst most puisant
Whom with thy wordes it easly had bin donne,
To make beleue both colde and darke the sonne.

Cruell, what offence hast thou for to bewayle,
The killing of thy loue if thou not repent?
If yee accompte so light of fayth to fayle :
What other sinne can make thy harte lament?
How treate you foes, if mee ye doo assayle ?
That loues thee so, with such cruell torment :
The heauens iustles, I will say to bee :
In case they shew the iust reuenge of mee.

If of offences all, that monstrous vice
Ingratitude, do most a man offend,
And if for that, an Angell of great price,
Was forced to Hell, from heauen to discend :
If great offence, great chastisment entice
When to reforme, the hart doth not him bend,
Take heed sharp skourge that God on thee not send
Thou art to mee vnkinde, and doost not mend.

If these also, besides some other spot
I haue (vnkinde) wherof thee to accuse,
That thou my hart with holdst, I meane it not,
I speake of thee that madest thee myne by lot,
And robbest mee since, against reaso which I must
Restore (vnkinde) for well thou wottest it playne,
They shalbe damned that others goods retaine.

                                        Vnkinde

Vnkinde, thou haſt forſaken mée, but I will
Not will thee willingly for none aſſayes
Yet this hard hap, and trouble for to flie,
I can and will, ende theſe my wofull dayes :
In onely way, in thy diſgrace to dye,
For if the Gods had graunted by their payes
My death, geuen then, when I ſtoode in thy grace,
No wight had dyed in halfe ſo happy a caſe.

### FINIS.

¶ The Louer vnto his Lady beloued,
of her disdaynfulneſſe toward him,

(might,

FOr beauties ſake though loue doth dread thy
And Venus thinks, by ſute to proue thy dame:
Though Pallas ſtriues, by hope of equall right,
For Wiſdoms watch, as daughter thée to claime.
Though Mercury would entitled be thy Syre,
For thy ſweet talke, ſo ſweetly blazed forth:
Though all the Gods, do burne in like deſire,
Thy graces rare, in heauen ſo much worth:
Yet lo, thy proofe I know, the truſty waight,
Of Tygars milke, thou foſtred wert from molde,
And Cipres Well with dainful chaung of fraight.
Gaue thee to drinke infected poyſon colde.
But yet beware, leaſt loue renew in thee,
The dreadfull flame Narciſſus whylom felt,
With eger moode, and ſight to feede thine eye.
Of thine owne, from others flame to ſwell:
For loue doth loue with hot reuenge to wreake,
The ruthles Iron hart, that will not breake.

### FINIS.

# The gorgious Gallery

Of shée for whom prowde Troy did fall and burne,
The Greekes eke slaine, that bluddy race did runne :
Nor shée for spight that did Acteon turne,
Into an Hart her beauty coye did shunne:
Nor shée whose blud vpon Achilles Tombe,
Whose face would tame a Tygars harte :
Nor shée that wan by wise of Paris dome.
Th'apple of Golde for Beauty to her parte :
Nor shée whose eyes did pearce true Troylus brest,
And made him yœld, that knew in loue no law,
Might bée compared to the fayrest and the best,
Whom Nature made to kéepe the rest in awe :
For Beauties sake, sent downe from Ioue aboue,
Thrise happy is hée, that can attayne her loue.

## FINIS.

¶ In the prayse of a beautifull and vertuous Virgin,
whose name begins with M.

(do leade
Behold you Dames ý raigne in fames, whose lookes mens harts
And triumph in the spoyle of those, vpō whose brests you trede.
A myrror make of M, whose molde, Dame Nature in disdayne,
To please her self, ɟ spight her foes, in beauty raysd to raigne:
Whose sunny beames ɟ starry eyes, presents a heauenlyke face,
And shewes the world a wonderous worke, sutch are her giftes of
In forhed, feature beareth, brunt in face doth fauor guyde,  (grace
In lookes is life, in shape is shame, in cheekes doth coulor hyde :
In boddy seemelynesse doth shew, in wordes doth wisdome shade,
All partes of her doth prayse deserue, in temprance is her trade.
In humble porte is honor platte, in face is maydens smyles
Her life is grafte with Golden giftes, her deedes deuoyd of gyles.
And

And as the Star to Marriners, is guyde vnto the Port,
So is this M, a heauenly ioy, to Louers that resort:
Who run and rome with inward wounds, & folded armes acrosse,
And hide their harms with clokes of care, & fæd their hope wᵗ losse.
Her lokes doth lift aboue the skyes, her frowns to Hel doth throw
All sues to her, shæ sekes on none, that daily proofe doth show:
Wherfore her saying late set forth, shæ burnt and could not flæ,
Though ment in prayse, yet far amis, I take it written bæ.
Shæ is none such as if shæ would, that any would disdayne :
But for the smartes of others græfes, of pitty shee did playne,
As one most lothe of any lyfe, for loue of her bee losse,
Or that with blud or cruell dædes, men write her beauties bosse:
For mercy is in M, her brest, and modest is her life,
A courtuous mayd, and like to prooue, a constant worthy wife.

## FINIS.

¶ The Louer deceyued by his Ladyes vnconstancy,
writeth vnto her as foloweth.

The heat is past that did mee fret,
The fier is out that nature wrought
The plantes of youth that I did set,
Are dry and dead within my thought
The Frost hath slayne the kindly sap,
That kept the hart in liuely state :
The sodayne storme and thunder clap :
Hath turned loue, to mortall hate.

The myst is gon that bleard mine eyes.
The lowring cloudes I see appeare,
Though that the blinde eate many flyes,
I would you knew, my sight is cleare:
Your sweete deceyuing flattryng face
Did make mee thinke that you were whiter

I muſe how you had ſuch a grace :
To ſæme a Hauke, and bæ a kyte.

Where precious ware is to be ſolde,
They ſhall it haue, that giueth moſt :
All things wæ ſæ, are won with Golde,
Few things is had, where is no coſt.
And ſo it fareth now by mæ,
Becauſe I preace to giue no gyftes:
Shæ takes my ſute vnthankfully,
And driues mæ of with many dryftes.

Is this th'end of all my ſute,
For my good will, to haue a ſkorne?
Is this of all my paynes the frute,
To haue the chaffe in ſteade of corne?
Let them that lyſt, poſſes ſuch droſſe,
For I deſerue a better gayne :
Yet had I rather leaue with loſſe,
Then ſerue and ſue, and all in vayne.

## FINIS.

¶ A true deſcription of Loue.

ſke what loue is? it is a paſſion,
Begun with reſt, and pampred vp in play :
Planted on ſight, and nouriſhed day by day,
With talke at large, for hope to graze vpon,
It is a ſhort ioy, long ſought, and ſœne gon:
An endles maze, wherin our willes do ſtray :
A gylefull gaine, repentance is the pay.
A great fier bred of ſmall occaſion,
A plague to make, our fraylty to vs knowen,
Where wæ therby, are ſubiecte to their lay :
Whoſe fraylty ought, to leaue vntill our ſtay,

In

# of gallant Inuentions.

In cafe our felues, this cuſtomé had not knowen.
Of hope and health, fuch creatures foʒ to pʒay,
Whofe gloʒy reſteth chæfly on denaye.

## FINIS.

¶ The Louer to his beloued, by the name
of fayre, and falfe.

O Cruell hart with falfehod infecte, of foʒce I muſt complayne,
Whofe poyfon hid, I may detect, as caufe doth mæ conſtrayn:
Thy name I ſhʒyne within my bʒeſt, thy dædes though I do tell,
No minde of malice I pʒoteſt, thy felfe doth know it well.
If thy deferts then bids mæ wʒite, I cannot well reuoke it,
I ſhall not fpare to ſhew thy fpite, I will no longer cloake it:
As Troylus truth ſhall bæ my ſhéeld, to kepe my pen from blame,
So Creſſids crafte ſhall kepe the fæld, foʒ to refound thy ſhame.
Vliſſes wife ſhall mate the foʒe, whofe wiſhly troth doth ſhine,
Well Fayʒe and Falfe, I can no moʒe, thou art of Helens lyne:
And daughter to Diana eke, with pale and deadly cheare,    yeare.
Whofe often chauāge I may well like, two mōnthes within the

## FINIS.

¶ The Louer defcribeth his paynfull plight, and
requireth fpeedy redreſſe, or prefent death.

The flaue of feruile foʒt, that boʒne is bond by kinde,
Doth not remayne in hope, w̄ fuch vnquiet minde:
Ne toſſed craſid Ship, with yʒkfome furging feas,
So grædely the quiet Poʒt, doth thirſt to ride at eafe.
As I thy ſhoʒt returne, with wiſhing bolwes require,
In hope that of my hatefull harmes, the date will then expire:
But time with ſtealing ſteps, and dʒiery dayes doth dʒiue,
And thou remaynſt then bound to come, if that thou bæ aliue.
Yy

O cruell Tygars whelpe, who had thy hand in holde?
When y with flattering pen thou wrotst, thy help at hand behold?
Beléeue it to bee true, I come without delay,
A foole and silly simple soule, yet dost thou still betray:
Whose moueles loue and trust, doth reason far surmount,
Whom Cupids trumpe, to fatall death hath sommond to accompt
My fayth and former life:fed with such frendly fier,
Haue not of thee by iust reward, deserued such falts hyer :
I promesse thee not mine, but thy case I bewayle,
What infamy may greater bee, then of thy fayth to fayle?
How ofte with humble sute? haue I besought the sonne, (to ronne?
That hee would spur his Coursers fearce, their race more swifte
To th'end with quicker speed, might come the promised day,
The day which I with louing lokes, and weary will did pray.
But thou art sure disposde to glory in my death,
Wherfore to feede thy fancy fond, loe, here I ende my breath,
I can not sighe nor sob, away by playnt I pine :
I see my fatall fainting file, ye Sisters do vntwine,
The Feriman I finde, prest at the Riuer side :
To take mee in his restles Boate, therin with him to ride.
And yet although I sterue, through thy dispitous fault:
Yet craue I not in my reuenge, that harme should thee assault,
But rather that thy fame, eternally may shine :
And that eche to thine auayle, aboundantly encline.
That eche thine enterprise, hath luckye lot and chaunce,
And stable fortune, thine estate, from day to day aduaunce,
That Sun, that Moone, that starres, and eke the plannets all,
The fier, the water, and the earth, may frendly to thee fal.
That many quiet yeres, thou number may with rest :
Uoyd of all annoyes and grieues , as may content thee best,
And if that foraine loue, torment and vere thy harte :
God yeeld thy weary wanting wish, and swagement of thy smart.
With froward stearing face, at mee if Fortune frowne,
Thou doost reioyce and I not so, but ioy thy good renowne:
And if I thée offend, for that I do thée loue,
Forgiue it mee:for force it is, I can it not remoue.

For I in secret sort, these lines to thee did I write,
My weakned wearied hand henssorth, shall sease for to endyte :
That letters to receiue from mee, thou neede not muse :
The messenger that next of all, of mee shal bring the newes.
Dissolued from the corps, shalbe my dolefull spright :        (sight,
That first (vnsheathd) shal passe to thee, when hee hath vewd thy
Contented hee shall go vnto the heauens aboue,
In case that ioyed rested place, may gayne it any loue.
And now for that my death, thy name may spot and stayne :
If that the flying fame therof, to others eares attayne,
I will not it were red, or knowen by other wayes :
That thou art only cause, I thus in ruthe dow ende my dayes.
Wherfore this Letter red, condemne it to the flame :
And if thou dow thy honnor forse, I know thou wilt thesame,
And if in lingring time, vnwares they chaunce to come :
Wherin the entrayles of the earth, shall hap to bee my tombe.
At least yet graunt mee this, it is a small request :
O happy wythered pyned corps, God send thy soule good rest.

## FINIS.

¶ The Lady beloued, assureth her Louer to bee his
owne, and not to change, while life doth last.

Deare hart as earst I was, so will I stil remayne,
Till I am dead, and more if more may bee:
Howsoeuer loue do yeeld mee ioy or payne,
Or Fortune lyst to smyle or frowne on mee
No chaunging chaunce my fast fayth may constrayne,
No more then Waues, or beating of the Sea
May stir the stedfast rocke, that will not ply,
For fayre nor fowle one inche, no more will I.
A file or knife of lead, shall sooner carue
The Diamant vnto what forme you will :
Ere Fortunes dynte, compell mee for to swarue,
Or the ire of Loue, to breake my constant will,

P iij                                       94

# The gorgious Gallery

Yœ sooner shall, the law of nature starue,
When Ryuers take their course agaynst the hill,
Ere sodayne hap, for better or for worse,
Disturne my thoughts, to take a better course.

With hartes consent, my loue you doo possesse,
A surer holde may chaunce, then many wéene :
The fayth by othe, that subiectes doo confesse,
To their new prince, is seldome stronger séene:
No fyrmer state than that, which loue doth sure exprette,
Of kinge, ne Keyser hitherto hath bén :
So that you néede not fortifie your hould,
With Towre or Ditch, least others win it should.

For though you set, no Souldiers for defence,
For all assaults, this one may yet suffise :
It is not goods can alter my pretence,
No gentle hart, yéeldes to so vile a prise,
Though crowne and septier, few would dispise,
Not beauty méete, to moue a wauering minde,
Yet more then yours, I wot not where to finde.

And feare you not, what forme my hart once tooke,
Least any new print, shall the same deface :
So déepe therin, ingraued is your looke,
As neuer may bée wyped from that place:
My hart like Waxe, so lightly did not broke,
More then one stroke, ere Cupid brought to passe
One splint of skale, therof to take away,
The best reserued, your Image to pourtray.

That like as what stone, it selfe best defendeth,
And hardiest is with toole to bee graue :
Doth sooner breake in péeces, then it bendeth,
To looze the stampe, afore my hand it gaue:
Euen so the nature, of my hart contendeth,
As hard is this, as any stone you haue :

                                        Though

## of gallant Inuentions.

Though fo2ce do b2eake it, vnto péeces small,
Those péeces somewhat, you resemble shall.

### FINIS.

¶ In the prayse of the rare beauty, and manifolde
vertues of Mistres D. as followeth.

IF Chawcer yet did lyue, whose English tongue did passe,
  Who sucked d2y Pernassus sp2ing, and raste the Iuice there was:
If Surrey had not scalde, the height of Ioue his Th2one,
Unto whose head a pillow softe, became Mount Helycon:
They with their Muses could, not haue p2onounst the same,
Of D. faire Dame, lo, a staming stock, the chéefe of natures frame.
They would but haue eclipsed, her beauties golden blast,
No2 Ouid yet of Poets P2ince, whose wits all others past.
Olde Nestor with his tongue, and flowing dew so swéete,
Would rather haue berefte her right, then pend her p2aises méete
In Helens heauenly face, whose grace the Greekes bought deare,
Fo2 whose defence p2owd Troy did fal, such fo2me did not appeare.
In Hectors sister loe : who Pirhus Father rapte,
Did not abound sutch beauty b2ight, as now to D, hath hapt :
Fo2 D, doth passe as far, Dame Venus with her p2ise,
As Venus did the other two, by doome of Paris wise.
If shée had p2esent bén, within the walles of Ide,
They would not had such disco2d then, no2 Paris iudgd that side.
In minde all voyd of doubt, they straight agréd would,
That D, should of god right, the Aple haue of Golde.
Whom as I must beléeue, that nature did create,
To rob the hartes of noble Kinge, and courage stoute to mate :
Her fo2head seemely spaste, wherin two shine her eyes,
No whit vnlike to starres by night, o2 beame when Phebus ryse.
Her haire that shines like golde, her shoulders couer whight,
To which no snow on Mountayne highe, may be compared right :
Her mouth well compast small, in smylings vtters fo2th
A treasure riche of O2ient Pearle, therto no Golde mo2e wo2th,

I

# The gorgious Gallery

I feare much Promethius fall, dare no further wade,
Whom loue embraced with the shape, that hee so finely made:
Yet this I dare presume, one thought of her may draw,
A harte of Iron, and it subdue, vnto blinde Cupids law.
I sorrow to recite, the bitter teares that flow:
Within the eyes of other Dames, that beauty know.
I weepe to wayle in minde, the burning flights that flame :
In troubled hartes of Natures case in spreading of her fame,
They all do curse themselues, of Nature makes complaynt,
That shee on them had smal regard, that did her thus depaynt.
Of her doth nobles spring, and sutors sue for grace,          (place,
And Fountaines eke of sugred speech, where voice can take no
Here Pallas should haue lost her prayse, for wisdome great,
Who gendred was of Ioue his braines, wher wisdom toke his seat.
Here wise Vlisses wyfe, whose chastnesse brued her fame :
Should matched bee, ye mated eke, in ventring of thesame.
Prowde Tarquin with his force, which Lucresse did defile :
Could not haue spoyled faire D. so , with neither sound nor gyle.
This Dame I thinke bee such, that heauen can vndermine,
And lifte the earth vnto the skyes, eche stone a star to shine.
If passed time (alas) might now returne agayne,
And all the wittes that euer was, would herein take the payne:
They could not at the ful, no due giftes expresse,
A wight vnfit to bee in earth, in heauen no such goddesse.
Whose name shall floorish still, though Atropos with spight:
In running from her deuelish Den, bereaue vs of this light,
Though Thesiphon do cut, her time of life a way :
Her cankred Swoord cannot assayle, her fame for to decay.
For wee in these our dayes, our selues may better quight :
To geue to her the cheefest prayse, then Paris which did right.
Lesse hatred cannot want, though power for to reuenge:
Our stately house as they did Troy, their force doth faile to senge.
Their might if it were like, these verses wee should rew,
With no lesse payne then Ouid did, whose greefe by Muses grew.

## FINIS.

Prety parables, and Prouerbes of Loue.

I Spake when I ment not, in ſpæding to gayne,
I ſought, when I ſped not, but trauaild in vayne :
I found where I feard not, would wꝛith wɨ the wind,
I loſte where I lou'd not, noꝛ foꝛſtɨ to finde.
  Nothing in which, truth is not truſtie,
But double is ſuch, and beauty but ruſtie :
I cæle with the colde, I leue that I like not,
I know not the olde, that rotteth and ripes not.
I fauoꝛ no ſuch, that fondly doth fauoꝛ,
I care not to much, foꝛ ſuch ſoꝛy ſauoꝛ :
I taſte oꝛ I try, in parte oꝛ in all,
I care not a fiye, the loſſe is but ſmall.
¶ laboꝛ at leaſure, I pꝛicke without payne,
In bſing foꝛ pleaſure, beates in my bꝛayne :
I ſpare not in byꝛding, to beat well the buſh,
Noꝛ leaue not in ſtryking, as long as they ruſh.
I try ere I truſt, nought waſting but winde,
Befoꝛe I finde iuſt, they know not my minde :
I iet not with Geminie, noꝛ tarry not with Tawre
In bluſtring who bleares mæ? I leaue them with Lawre.
Foꝛ fier who fyndeth, in burning to bight,
The wiſe man hæ warneth, to leape from the light :
Foꝛ ſæing the wæde, and loſing from bandes,
The plowing in Sea, and ſowing in Sandes.

**FINIS.**

I                                                    Of

# The gorgious Gallery

### Of patience.

A Soueraygne salue there is for eche disease:
  The cheefe reuenge for cruell ire
Is pacience, the cheefe and present ease,
  For to delay eche yll desire.

### Of lawlesse lust.

AN euerlasting bondage doth hee chuse,
  That can not tell a litle how to vse:
Hee scant ynough for shame puruayes,
  That all alone to lust obayes.

### Of will, and reason.

I Count this conquest great,
  That can by reasons skill:
Subdue affectious heate,
  And vanquish wanton will.

### Of three things to be shunned.

THree thinges, who seekes for prayse, must flye,
  To please the taste with wine
Is one: another, for to lye
  Full softe on fethers fine.
The thirde and hardest for to shunne,
  And cheefest to eschew,
Is lickerous lust, which once begun,
  Repentance doth ensue.

### Of beauty, and chastity.

CHastity a vertue rare,
  Is seldome knowen to run her race:
Where cumly shape and beauty faire,
  Are seene to haue a byding place.

### Of wisdome.

WHo seeketh the renowne to haue,
  And eke the prayse of Uertues name:
Of Wisdome rare hee ought to craue,
  With gladsome will to worke the same.

### Of a pure conscience.

A Conscience pure withouten spot,
   That knoweth it selfe for to bee free :
Of slaunders lothsome reketh not,
A brazen wall full well may bee.

### Of frendship founde by chaunce.

The frendship found by chaunce is such,
   As often chaunce is seene to chaunge :
And therfore trust it not to much,
Ne make therof a gaine to straunge :
For proofe hath taught by hap is had,
Sometime as well the good as bad.

### Of good will got by due desert.

But I suppose the same good will,
   That once by good desart is got :
That fancy findes by reasons skill,
And time shall try withouten spot ,
Is such as harde is to bee gayned,
And worthy got to bee retayned.

### Of flatterers and faythfull friendes.

The finest tongue can tel the smoothest tale,
   The hottest fiers haue ofte the highest smoke :
The hardiest knightes the consst will assaile,
The strongest armes can giue the sturdest stroke
The wysest men be thought of greatest skill,
And poorest frendes be found of most good will.

### Of a vertuous , life, age, and death.

God wot my frend our life full soone decayes,
   And vertue voydes no wrinkels from the face :
Approching age by no entreatie stayes,
And death vntamed, will graunt no man grace.

FINIS.

A proper Posie for a Handkercher.

*Fancy is fearce, Desire is bolde,*
*will is wilfull, but Reason is colde.*

K
¶ The

# The gorgious Gallery

¶ The Louer beeing ouermuch weryed with seruile
lyfe, compareth it to a Laborinth.

WIth speedy winges, my fethered woes pursues,
My wretched life, made olde by weary dayes:
But as the fire of Æthna stil renues,
And breedes as much, by flame as it decayes:
Myh eauy cares, that once I thought would ende mœ,
Prolongs my life, the moze mishap to lende mœ.

Oh haples will, with such vnwary eyes,
About mishap that hast thy selfe bewzethed:
Thy trust of weale, my wailfull prase dcayes,
To wofull state wherby I am bequethed:
And into such a Labozinth betake,
As Dedalus foz Minotaure did make.

With helples search, wheras it were, assinde,
Without reuoke, I tread these endles Mayes:
Where moze I walke, the moze my selfe I winde.
Without a guyde, in Tozments tzzing wayes:
In hope I dzead, where to and fro I rome,
By death ne life, and findes no better bome.

But sithe I sœ, that sozzow cannot eyde,
These haples howzes, the lines of my mischance:
And that my hope, can nought a whit amend,
My bitter dayes, noz better hap aduance:
I shall shake of, both doubtfull hope and dzede,
And so bee pleased, as God is best agrœde.

## FINIS.

## How to choose a faythfull freende.

Though that my yeares, full far two ſtande aloofe,
From counſell ſage, or Wiſdomes good aduice :
What I doo know by ſoone repenting proofe,
I ſhall you tell, and learne if you be wiſe.
From finœd wits, that telles the ſmootheſt tale,
Beware, their tongues doo flatter oſt a wry :
A modeſt loke ſhall well ſet forth your ſale,
Truſt not to much, before ſomewhat you try :
So guyde your ſelfe in worde, and eke in dœde,
As bad and good may prayſe your ſober name :
Aſſay your frœnd, before your greateſt neede,
And to conclude, when I may doo that ſame,
That may you pleaſe, and beſt content your minde,
Aſſure your ſelfe, a faythfull frœnd to finde.

## FINIS.

### The Louer beeing accuſed of ſuſpicion of flattery, pleadeth not gyltie, and yet is wrongfully condemned.

To ſœme for to reuenge, eche wrong in haſtie wiſe,
By proofe wœ ſœ of gyltleſſe men, it hath not bin the guiſe :
In ſlaunders lothſome brute ; when they condemned bee,
With rageles moodes they ſuffer wronge, when truth ſhall fry
Theſe are the pacient panges, y pas within the breſt (them frœ :
Of thoſe that feele their caſe by mine, where wrong hath right
I know how by ſuſpect, I haue bean indged away, (oppreſt :
And graunted gyltie in the thing, that clearly I denye.
My fayth may mee defende, if I might leuid bœ,
God iudge mee ſo, as from that gylte I know mee to bee free :
I wrought but for my freend, the greefe was all mine owne,
As if the troth were truely tryde, by prooft it might be knowne.
Yet are there ſuch that ſay, they ran my meaning deeme,
Without reſpect to this olde troth: things proue not as they ſeeme:

Wherby

Wherby it may befall, in iudgment to bee quicke,
To make them be suspecte therwith, that nædeth not to kicke:
Yet in resisting wrong, I would not haue it thought,
I dow accuse as though I knew, by whom it may be wrought:
If any such there bæ that herewithall be vext,
It were their vertue to beware, and deeme mee better nexte.

### FINIS.

### The Louer describeth the daungerous state of Ambition.

Eholde these high and mighty men,
Their chaunging state and tell mee then:
Where they or wee, best dayes doo see,
Though wee seeme not and they to bee
    In wealth.
Their pleasant course straung traces hath,
On tops of trees that groundles path:
    Full waueringly.
For bee it calme they tread not fast,
Blow roughe, blow soft, all helpe is past:
    Appearingly.
With vs, ye see, it is not so,
That clime not vp, but kepe below:
In calmes our course is faire and playne,
Huge hilles defendes from stormy rayne:
    For why?
The raging winde and stormy showcr,
On mountaynes high it hath most power
    Naturally.
But wee that in lowe valleis lye,
Beholde may such as wander bye:
    So spdingly:
Then what is hee that will aspire,
To heape such woe to please desire:

               That

# of gallant Inuentions.

That may in wealth by staying still,
Spend well his dayes and fly from yll:
　　　To good.
By hauing his recourse to God
To loue his lawes so feare his rod:
　　　Unfaynedly.
To doo that in his worde wee finde,
To helpe the poore, the sicke, the blinde:
　　　Accordingly.
But though gaynsayd this can not bée,
Deeme men by deedes, and yee shall see:
That these low valleies they can not bide,
But vp will clyme, though downe they slyde:
　　　Agayne.
The poore the riche mans place doth craue,
The riche would fayne hyer places haue:
　　　Ambiciously.
The Squyre, the knight, a Lorde would bée,
The Lorde, the Erle would hyer then hée:
　　　Full dangerously.
When these attayne to their desire,
Then meaner men are set on fire:
To haue the roomes which they in wers,
So that ye see all times some there:
　　　In hart.
When one is gon, another is come,
The third catching the secondes roome:
　　　Full speedely.
Thus clyming one to others tayle,
The bowes either breake, or footing fayle:
　　　Full totteringly.
For when the top they haue attaynd,
And got is all they would haue gaynd:
Then downe they come wit sodayne fall,
In doubtfull case of life and all.
　　　And thus.

　　　　　I iiii　　　　　Ambition

# The gorgious Gallery

Ambition reapeth worthy hyre,
Becaufe hæ would fuch fporte afpyre
Unequally.
And there his bragge is layd full low,
That thought on hie, himfelf to fhow.
Deferuedly.

## FINIS.

The paynfull plight of a Louer remayning in doubtfull
hope of his Ladyes fauour.

The bitter fwæte, that ftraynes my yælded harte,
  The careleffe count, which doth the fame imbrace:
The doubtfull hope, to reape my due dezart,
The penfiue pathe, that guides my reftles race:
Are at fuch war, within my wounded breft,
As doth bereaue, my ioy and eke my reft.

My grædy will, which feekes the golden gayne,
My luckles lot, doth alwayes take in worth :
My matched minde, that dreades my futes in bayne,
My pittious playnt, doth helpe for to fet forth :
So that betwixt, two waues of raging Seas,
I driue my dayes, in troubles and difeafe.

My wofull eyes, doo take their chæfe delight,
To fæde their fill, vpon their pleafant maze :
My hidden harmes, that grow in mæ by fight,
With pyning panges, doo driue mee from the gaze:
And to my hap, I reape none other hire,
But burne my felfe, and I to blow the fire.

## FINIS.

# of gallant Inuentions.

The Louer recounteth his faythfull diligence towarde
his beloued, with the rewardes that
hee reapeth therof.

My fancy fæ∂es, vpon the sugred gaule,
My witlesse will, vnwillingly wo2kes my woe :
My carefull choyse, ∂oth chose to kæpe mæ th2aule,
My franticke folly, fawns vpon my foe :
My lust alluers, my lickering lyppes to tafte,
The bayte wherin, the subtill hooke is plafte.

My hungry hope, ∂oth heape my heauy hap,
My sund2y sutes, p2ocure my mo2e dif∂ayne :
My stea∂fast steppes, yet sly∂e into the trap,
My try∂ truth, entangleth mæ in trayne :
I spye the snare, and will not backward go,
My reason yæl∂es, and yet sayth euer, no.

In pleasant plat, I trea∂ vpon the snake,
My flamyng thirst, I quench with venomd Wine :
In vayntie dish, I ∂ω the poyson take,
My hunger bid∂es mæ, rather eate then pine :
I sow, I set, yet fruit, ne flow2e I fin∂e,
I p2icke my hand, yet leaue the Rosebehin∂e.

## FINIS.

A                    ¶ A Letter

# The gorgious Gallery

¶ A Letter written by a yonge gentilwoman and sent to her
husband vnawares (by a freend of hers) into Italy.

Imagine when these blurred lines, thus scribled out of frame,
  Shall come before thy careles eyes, for thee to read the same:
To bee through no default of pen, or els through prowd disdayne,
But only through surpassing græfe, which did the Author payne
Whose quiuering hand could haue no stay, this carsul bil to write
Through flushing teares distilling fast, whilst shee did it indite:
Which teares perhaps may haue some force (if thou no tigre bee,
And mollifie thy stony hart, to haue remorse on mee.
Ah periurde wight reclaime thy selfe, and saue thy louing mate,
Whom thou hast left beclogged now, in most vnhappy state:
(Ay mee poore wench) what luckles star? what frowning god aboue
What hellish hag? what furious fate hath changd our former loue?
Are wee debard our wonted ioyes? shall wee no more embrace?
Wilt thou my deare in country strang, ensue Eneas race:
Italians send my louer home, hee is no Germayne borne,
Vnles ye welcome him because hee leaues mee thus forlorne.
As earst ye did Anchises sonne, the founder of your soyle,
Who falsely fled from Carthage Queene, releuer of his toyle:
Oh send him to Bryttannia Coastes, vnto his trusty fære,
That shee may vew his cumly corps, whom shee estemes so deere:
Where wee may once againe renue, our late surpassed dayes,
Which then were spent with kisses sweet, & other wanton playes:
But all in vayne (forgiue thy thrall, if shee do iudge awrong)
Thou canst not want of dainty Trulles Italian Dames among.
This only now I speake by gesse, but if it happen true,
Suppose that thou hast seene the sword, that mee thy Louer slue:
Perchance through time so merrily with dallying damsels spent,
Thou standst in doubt & wilte enquire from whom these lines were
If so, remember first of all, if thou hast any spowse,     (sent:
Remember when, to whom and why, thou earst hast plited vowes,
Remember who estemes thee best, and who bewayles thy flight.
Minde her to whom for loyalty thou falshood dost requight.

                            Remember

of gallant Inuentions.

Remember Heauen, forget not Hell, and way thyne owne eſtate,
Reuoke to minde whom thou haſt left, in ſhamefull blame & hate:
Yea minde her well who did ſubmit, into thine onely powre,
Both hart and life, and therwithall, a ritch and wealthy dowre:
And laſt of all which greeues mee moſt, that I was ſo begylde,
Remember moſt forgetfull man, thy pretty tatling childe:
The leaſt of theſe ſurnamed things, I hope may well ſuffiſe,
To ſhew to thee the wretched Dame, that did this bill deuiſe.
I ſpeake in vayne, thou haſt thy will, and now ſayth Aeſons ſonne,
Medea may packe vp her pypes, the golden Fleeſe is wonne:
If ſo, be ſure Medea I will, ſhew forth my ſelfe in deede,
Yet gods defend though death I taſte, I ſhould diſtroy thy ſeede:
Agayne, if that I ſhould enquire, wherfore thou dwſt ſoiurne,
No anſwere fitly mayſt thou make, I know to ſerue thy turne:
Thou canſt not ſay but that I haue, obſeru'd my loue to thæ,
Thou canſt not ſay, but that I haue, of life vnchaſt bin fræ. (bound
Thou canſt not cloak (through want) thy flight, ſince riches did a
Thou nædes not ſhame of mæ thy ſpouſe, whoſe byrth not low is
As for my beauty, thou thy ſelf, earwhile didſt it commend (found,
And to conclude I knew no thing, wherin I dyd offend:
Retier with ſpæd, I long to ſee, thy barke in wiſhed bay,
The Seas are calmer to returne, then earſt to fly away.
Beholde the gentill windes dw ſerue, ſo that a frendly gayle,
Would ſwne conuay to happy Porte, thy moſt deſired ſayle:
Return would make amends for all, and banniſh former wronge,
Oh that I had for to entice, a Scyrens flattering ſonge.
But out alas, I haue no ſhift, or cunning to entreat,
It may ſuffiſe in abſence thine, that I my griæfes repeate
Demaund not how I did diſgeſt, at firſt thy ſodayne flight,
For ten dayes ſpace I twke no reſt, by day nor yet by night:
But like to Baccus beldame Nonne, I ſent and rangde apace,
To ſæ if that I mought thæ finde, in ſome frequented place:
Now here, now there, now vp, now down, my fancy ſo was fed,
Untill at length I knew of troth, that thou from mee wert fled.
Then was I fully bent with blade, to ſtab my vexed harte,
Yet hope that thou wouldſt come agayn, my purpoſe did conuart:

K y                                                    And

# The gorgious Gallery

And so ere since I liu'd in hope bemirt with dzeadful feare,
My smeared face through endles teares, vnpleasant doth appeare:
My slepes vnsound with vgly dreams, my meats are vayn of taste
My gozgious rayment is dispiloe, my tresses rudly plaste,
And to bee bzeefe: I bouldly speake, there doth remayne no eare:
But that therof in amplest wise, I dø possesse a share:
Lyke as the tender spzig doth bend, with euery blast cf winde,
Oz as the guidelesse Ship on Seas, no certaine Pozte may finde.
So I now subiecte vnto hope, now thzall to carefull dzead,
Amids the Rocks, tween hope and feare, as fancy moues, am led:
Alas returne, my deare returne, returne and take thy rest,
God graunt my wozdes may haue the force, to penetrat thy bzest.
What dost thou thinke in Italy, some great exployt to win?
No, no, it is not Italy, as sometimes it hath bin:
Oz dost thou loue to gad abzoad, the fozrain costes to vew,
If so, thou hadst not døne amisse, to bid mee first a dew:
But what hath bin the cause, I nede not descant longe,
Foz sure I am, meane while poze wench, I only suffer wzong.
Wel thus I leaue, yetmoze could say: but least thou shouldst refuse,
Through tediousnesse to rede my lines, the rest I will excuse:
Untill such time as mighty Ioue dothsend such luckye grace,
As wee therof in frendly wise, may reasomface to face.
Till then farwell, and bee thee kepe, who only knowes my smart,
And with this bill I send to thee, a trusty Louers harte.

By mee, to thee, not mine, but thine,
  Since Loue doth moue the same,
Thy mate, though late, doth wright, her plight,
  Thou well, canst tell, her name.

# of gallant Inuentions.

¶ A Letter sent from beyond the Seaes to his Louer, perswading
her to continew her loue towardes him.

TO thée I write whose life and death, thy faith may saue or spil :
Which fayth obserue, I liue in ioy, if not, your frend you kill:
Suspecte not that I do misdoubt, your loyalty at all :
But ponder how that louers are, vnto suspicion thrall.
Which thraldome brédeth furth thrall, if wonted fayth do fayle :
Agaynst the Louer thus forlorne, do thousand Cares preuayle :
It litle helpes to haue begun, and there to set a stay,
They win more fame, that fight it out : then those that run away.
Like as the willing hound that doth, pursue the Deare in Chace :
Will not omit vnto the ende, his paynfull weary race :
So Loue (if loue it bée indéd) will stedfast still remayne:
What so betide, good hap or yll, and not reuoult agayne.
Such fayth of you, swéet hart I aske, such fayth: why sayd I so ?
What néde I to demaund the thing, I haue had long ago :
Your fayth you gaue, the case is playn, you may not séeme to starf:
And I in earnest of the match did leaue with you my hart.
But now perhaps you may alleage, long distance may procure,
A cause wherby our former loue, no longer may endure :
If so you Iudge to far amisse, although that sayle and winde,
Conuay my corps to cuntry strange, my hart remaynes behinde.
Examples many could I shew, but néedles is that payne,
Mine owne example shall suffise, when I returne agayne :
Meane while although to swim I want, Leanders cunning art,
In all things els (except the same) Ile play Leanders part.
In hope that thou wilt shew thy selfe, to mée an Hero true,
And so although loth to depart, I say swéete hart adue.

A Ringe I sende, wherin is pende, a Posie (if you reede)
Wherby you may, perceaue alway, of what I most haue néede.
By mee your frende, vnto the ende, if you therto agree,
Although not so, your louing foe, I still perforce must bee.

## FINIS.

L.iii.                    Another

# The gorgious Gallery

## An other louing Letter.

BEcause my hart is not mine owne, but resteth now with thée,
I greet thée well of hartinesse, thy selfe mayst Caruer bée:
Muse not hereat but like hereof, first read and then excuse,
I wish to you a plyant hart, when you these lines peruse. (boulde,
Hope bids me speak, fear stayes my tongue, but Cupid makes mée
And Fancy harps of good successe, when that my playnt is tould:
Thus Hope doth prick, & feare doth kicke, & fancy féds my brayn,
In you alone doth now consist, the salue to ease my payne.
You are my Paradice of ioy, the heauen of my delight,
And therwithall (which thing is strang) the worker of my spight:
Which spight I séeke not to reuenge, but méekely to subdue,
Not as a foe, but as a friend, I do your loue pursue.
I yeeld my selfe vnto your power, and will not you relente?
In humble wise I mercy craue, and is your mercy spente?
No sure, as nature outwardly, hath shewde in you her skill,
I doubt not but that inwardly, the like shee doth fulfill.
So good a face, so trim a grace, as doth in you remayne:
A Cressids cruell stony harte, I know may not retayne:
Wherfore to ratefie my wordes, let déedes apparant bée:
Then may you vaunt and proue it true, you fréedom gaue to mée.
Consider of my restles care, and way blinde Cupids ire:
Then shal you finde my paynful loue, doth claym but earned hire.
Requite not this my curtesy, and fréendship with disdaine,
But as I loue vnfainedly, so yéld like loue againe.
Allow hereof as for the rest, that doth belong to loue:
My selfe therof will take the care, as time, in time shall proue.
Meane while, I wish a Thisbies hart, in you there may endure:
Then doubt not, but a Pyramus, of mée you shall procure.

Yours at your will,
To saue or spill.

FINIS.

# Pretie pamphlets, by T. Proctor.

## Proctors Precepts.

LEaue vading plumes, no more vaunt, gallant youth,
Thy masking weeds forsake, take collours sage:
Shun vicious steps, consider what ensueth,
Time lewdly spent, when on coms crooked age.
When beauty braue shall vade, as doth the flower,
When manly might, shall yeeld to auncient time:
When yonge delightes shall dye, and ages bower,
Shall lodge thy corps, bemoning idle prime.
Learne of the Ant, for stormy blastes to get
Prouision, least vntimely want do cum,
And moues thee mone such time, so lewd neglect
From vertues lore, where worthy honors wun.
Thinke how vncertayne here, thou liust a guest,
Amid such vice, thats irksome to beholde:
Thinke whence thou camst, and where thy corps shall rest,
When breathing breath, shall leaue thy carkasse colde.
When dreadfull death, shall daunt thy hauty minde,
When fearfull flesh, shall throwd in clammy clay:
When pamperd plumes shall vade, and dreads shall finde,
Deseruings due, for erring lewd astray.
Run not to rash, least triall make the mone,
In auncient yeres thy greene vnbridled time:
Olde Age is lothd, with folly ouer grown,
Yonge yeres dispisde, cut of in sprowting prime.
Experience learne, let elder lyues thee lead,
In lyuely yeres, thy fickle steps to guide:
Least vnawares, such vncoth paths thou tread,
Which filthy be thought, pleasant to be eyde.
In calmest Seas, the deepest Whorepooles bee,
In greenest Grasse, the lurking Adder lyes:
With eger sting, the sugerest sap wee see,
Smooth wordes deceiue, learne therfore to bee wise.

FINIS.

# The gorgious Gallery

*Inuidus alterius rebus macrescit opimis.*

THe greedy man, whose hart with hate doth swell,
Because hee sees his neyghbors good estate :
Liues vncontent, with what might serue him well,
And eftsoones seemes to blame sufficient fate :
This grudging gluton glut, with goulden gayne,
To serue his vse, although hee hath enough :
Repines at that, which others get with payne,
So that himselfe therby, hee doth abase :
Yee thinkes that much, which passeth by his claw,
And findes a fault for it through luckles hap :
Although the matter valueth scarce a straw,
Yee deemes it small of gaine, that giues no sap.
Yee thinkes his store, shall serue his senclesse corse,
Or that no death at all, hee deemes there bee :
Els would hee to his conscience haue remorse,
And seeke to liue content with his degree :
For what auayles, to horde vp heapes of drosse,
Or seeke to please vnsaciate fond desire :
Considering that, tis subiect vnto losse,
And wee (therby yll got) deserues Hell fire :
From which O Lord conduct vs with thy hand,
And giue vs grace to liue vnto thy prayse :
Preserue our Queene his subiects and her land,
And graunt in peace, shee raigne here Nestors dayes.

## FINIS.

## The reward of Whoredome by the fall of Helen.

From Limbo Lake, where dismall fœndes do lye,
Where Pluto raignes, perpend Helenas cry :
Where firy flames, where pittious howlings bee,
Where bodyes burne: from thence giue eare to mee.
I am Helena shœ, for whose vilde filthy fact,
The stately Towers of Troy, the hauty Grecians sacte :
High Troy, whose pompe, throughout the world did sound,
In Cinders low, through mee was layd on ground .
Kinge Priamus through mœ, did end his life :
And Troians all almost, I was the cause of strife.
I am that Dame, whose beauty passing braue,
Dame Venus praysde, the golden Pome to haue :
Whose feature forste, Sir Paris boyling brest,
To leaue his land, and sœke to be my guest.
That trull which tost, the surging Seas a maine,
From Grecian shoare, to Troy vnto my paine.
That slurt, whose gallant sproutinge prime,
Through vilde abuse, was scorcht ere auncient time:
I vertue shund, I lothd a modest mynde,
I wayd not fame, my beauty made mee blinde.
Each braue delight, my masking minde allurde,
My fancy dœmed, my beauties gloze assurde :
Such worthy fame, did sound of Helens hue,
Although my dœdes, reapt shame, and guerdon due.
In gorgious plumes, I maskt, puft vp with pride,
In braue delights I liu'd, my fancy was my guide :
But fie of filth, your world is all but vayne,
Your pomp cousumes, your deeds shall guerdon gaine :
See here by mee, whose beauty might haue boast,
For splendaut hue, throughout each forrain coast.
But what preuayles, to vaunt of beauties gloze,
Or brag of pride, wheron dishonor growes :
If I had vsde my gifts in vertues lore,
And modest liud, my prayse had bin the more.

L                                    Where

# The gorgious Gallery

Where now too late, I lothe my life lewd spent,
And wish I had, with vertue bin content.

FINIS.     T. P.

### A Louers lyfe.

The tedious toyle, the cares which Louers taste, (feare:
The troubled thoughts, which moues their mindes to
The pinching pangs, the dole which seemes to waste,
Their lothsome life, deepe plungd in gulfes of care:
 Would mooue ech shun, such snares of vayne delight,
 Which irksome be, though pleasant to the sight.

The minde full fraught, with care enioyes no ease,
A boyling brest, desires vnlawfull lust:
The hart would haue, what best the minde doth please,
And fancy craues, the thing which is vniust.
 Beside eche frown, which eftsoones moues them deeme,
 They abiect are, if sad their Louers seeme.

Or if occasion shun, their vsuall sight,
Not seene, they thinke themselues vnminded bee:
And then in dumps, as mazd they leaue delight,
And yeeld to graefe, till one, eche others see:
 So that with feare, their mindes are alwayes fraught,
 That liue in loue, experience some hath taught.

Eche lowring frown, from mirth doth moue the minde,
One iesting worde, procures a thousand woes:
So that lyke graefe or more, through sight they finde,
Then absence sure, such cares fro fancy flowes:
 Such goring gripes, such heapes of hideous harmes,
 Such sorowing sobs, from daunted louers swarmies.

Rosamond a spowsed Dame, her husbands death procurde,
For speaking but a worde in iest:
Itrascus too, full thyrty yeares indurde,
The panges of loue, within his boyling brest:     (care,
 So that in graefe they harbor, still their mindes are cloyd with
 They diue in dole, they plunge in payne, & liue in cruell feare.

And

## of gallant Inuentions.

And diuers moe, as Axeres whofe beauty paſſing faire,
So Iphis hart, and boyling breſt allurde :
That for her ſake, hée liude in extreame care,
And cruell grǽfe, while breathing breath indurde :
But at the length, diſdayne vpon a trǽ,
Hǽ honge himſelfe, where ſhǽ his corps might ſǽ.

### FINIS.

¶ A Louer approuing his Lady vnkinde.
Is forſed vnwilling to vtter his minde.

Willow willow willow, ſinge all of grǽne willow,
Sing all of grǽne willow, ſhall bǽ my Garland.

My loue, what miſlyking in mǽ do you finde,
  Sing all of grǽne willow :
That on ſuch a ſoddayn, you alter your minde,
  Sing willow willow willow :
What cauſe doth compell you, ſo fickle to bǽ?
  Willow willow willow willow :
In hart which you plighted, moſt loyall to mǽ,
  Willow willow willow willow.

I faythfully ſwed, my fayth to remayne,
  Sing all of grǽne willow :
In hope I as conſtant, ſhould finde you agayne,
  Sing willow willow willow :
But periurde as Iaſon, you faythleſſe I finde,
Which makes mee vnwilling, to vtter my minde :
  Willow willow willow, ſinge all of grǽne willow,
  Sing all of greene willow ſhall bee my Garland.

Your beauty braue decked, with ſhowes gallant gay,
  Sing all of greene willow :
Allured my fancy, I could not ſay nay,
  Sing willow willow willow.

L ij                    Peaſe

Your phrases fine philed, did force mée agrée,
Willow willow willow willow :
In hope as you promis'd, you loyall would bée,
Willow willow willow willow.

But now you be frisking, you list not abide,
Sing all of græne willow :
Your vow most vnconstant, and faythlesse is tride,
Sing willow, willow willow :
Your wordes are vncertayne, not trusty you stand,
Which makes mée to weare, the willow Garland :
 Willow willow willow, sing all of græne willow,
 Sing all of græne willow, shall bée my Garland.

Hath Light of loue luld you, so softe in her lap?
Sing all of græne willow :
Hath fancy prouokte you, did loue you intrap?
Sing willow willow willow :
That now you be flurting, and will not abide.
Willow willow willow willow :
To mée which most trusty, in time should haue tride,
 Willow willow willow willow.

Is modest demeanure, thus turnd to vntrust?
Sing all of græne willow :
Are fayth and troth fixed, approoued vniust?
Sing willow, willow will :
Are you shée which constant, for euer would stand?
And yet will you giue mée, the willow Garland?
 Willow willow willow, singe all of græne willow,
 Sing all of græne willow, shall bée my Garland.

What motion hath moude you, to maske in delight,
Sing all of græne willow,
What toy haue you taken, why séeme you to spight
Sing willow willow willow,

                                        Your

# of gallant Inuentions.

Your loue which was ready foz aye to indure,
    Willow willow willow willow :
Accozding to pzomise most constant and sure,
    Willow willow willow willow.

What gallant you conquerd, what youth mœude your minds,
    Sing all of græne willow :
To leaue your olde Louer, and bée so vnkinde,
    Singe willow willow willow :
To him which you plighted both fayth, troth and hand,
Foz euer: yet giues mee the willow Garland ?
      Willow willow willow, singe all of greene willow,
      Sing all of greene willow, shall bee my Garland.

Hath wealth you allured, the which I dœ want,
    Sing all of greene willow :
Hath pleasant deuises, compeld you recant,
    Sing willlow willow willow :
Hath feature fozste you, your wozds to deny?
    Willow willow willow willow :
Oz is it your fashion to cog, and to lye,
    Willow willow willow willow ?

What are your sweet smiles, quite turnd into lowres,
    Sing all of greene willow :
Oz is it your ozder, to change them by howzes,
    Sing willow willow willow :
What haue you sufficient, thinke you in your hand,
To pay foz the making, of my willow Garland :
      Willow willow willow, singe all of greene willow,
      Sing all of greene willow, shall bee my Garland.

Farewell then most fickle, vntrue and vniust,
    Sing all of greene willow :
Thy deedes are yll dealings, iu thee is no trust,
    Willow willow willow willow.

Thy bowes are vncertayne, thy wordes are but winde
  Willow willow willow willow.
God graunt thy new louer, more trusty thee finde,
  Willow willow willow willow?

Be warned then gallants, by proofe I vnfolde,
  Sing willow willow willow,
Mayds loue is vncertayne, soone hot, and soone colde,
  Sing willow willow willow:
They turne as the reed, not trusty they stand,
Which makes mee to weare the willow Garland:
  Willow willow willow, singe all of greene willow,
  Sing all of greene willow, shall bee my Garland.

### FINIS.

### A gloze of fawning freendship.

NOw cease to sing your Syren songes, I leaue ech braue delight
  Attempt no more the wounded corps, which late felt fortunes spight:
But rather helpe to rue, with sorowing sobs come mone,
My lucklesse losse from wealth to woe, by fickle fortune throwne.
I once had freends good store, for loue, (no drosse I tryde)
For hauing lost my goods on Seas, my freends would not abide,
Yet hauing neede I went to one, of all I trusted moste:
To get releefe, hee answerd thus, go packe thou peuish posse.
His wordes did pearce my tender brest, and I as mazde did stand
Requesting him with pitteous plaints, to giue his helping hand:
Content thy selfe (quoth hee) to serue my owne estate,
I haue not I, yet am I greeu'd to see thy lucklesse fate.
Ah fie of fawning freends, whose eyes attentiue bee,
To watch and warde for lukers sake, with cap and bended knee:
Would God I had not knowne, their sweet and sugered speach,
Then had my greefe the lesser bin, experience mee doth teach.

### FINIS.

## A Maze of Maydens.

Ho goes to gaze of euery gallant girle,
And castes his eyes at euery glauncing gloze :
Whose masking minde, with euery motion mou'd,
In fine shall finde, his fancy fraught with woes.

For pleasure spent, is but a wishing vayne,
By crooked chaunce, depriude of braue delight :
Cut of by care, a heape of hurtfull harmes,
Our gaze vngaynd, which whilome pleasde our sight.

Our vaunts doo vade, our pleasures passe away,
Our sugerest swætes, reapes sorowing sobs in fine :
Our braggest boast, of beauties brauest blaze,
To sorowed browes, doth at the length resigne.

Our foolish fancy filde, with filthy vice,
Pursues his hurt, vnto anothers harmes :
A houering hart, with euery gloze enticed,
gaynes lothsome loue, whence nought but sorow swarmes.

Leaue then to gaze, of euery glauncing gloze,
Contemne the sleights, of beauties sugerest bate :
Whose outward sheath, with colours braue imbost,
Shuns cruell craft, and enuious hurtfull hate.

### FINIS.

# The gorgious Gallery

A short Epistle written in the behalfe of N. B. to M. H.

Eare Lady deckt with cumlynesse,
To counteruayle my clemency :
Bée prest, I pray, in readynesse,
To yeeld your courteous curtesse.

Let mee you finde Penelope,
In minde, and loyall hart :
So shall I, your Vlisses bée,
Till breathing lyfe depart.

Yelde loue for loue, to him who lykes,
To liue in lynckes of loyalty :
And graunt him grace, who nothing séekes,
For his good will, but curtesy.

Let mee your bondman, fauour finde,
To gratesie my willing harte :
Whom no attempt, to please your minde,
Shall hynder mee, to play my parte.

Permit mee not, in lingring sorte,
To labour in a barrayn soyle :
Ne giue occasion to reporte,
How loytryng loue, reapes troubled toyle.

But let mee say, my hart obtaynd,
The gloze, which pleasd my glauncing eyes :
And that I haue for guerdon gaynd,
The best that in my Lady lyes.

So shall I boast of that, which best
Doth please the prime of my desire :
And glory in a gayned rest,
Which through your fauour I aspire.
FINIS.

## A vew of vayn glory.

What motion moze,may moue a man to minde
His owne eſtate,then pzoue,whoſe dayes vnſure,
Accounted are vnto a puffe of winde,
A bzeathing blaſt,whoſe force can not endure :
Whoſe lyuely ſhowes conſumes,whoſe pompe decayes,
Whoſe glozy dyes,whoſe pleaſures ſoone be ſpent :
Whoſe ſtouteſt ſtrength,to weakenes ſubiect ſtayes,
Whoſe thoughts bee vaine,and vade as though vnment.
What haue wee then to vaunt,oz glozy in?
Sith all is vayne,wherin wee take delight :
Why ſhould wee boaſt oz bzag,ſith nought wee win
In fine, but death?to whom yældes euery wight.
To equall ſtate,bee bzingeth each degræe,
Hæ feareth none,all ſubiects yældes to death :
To dankiſh duſt,hæ dziueth all wee ſæ,
Which in the wozld,enioyeth any bzeath :
Why vaunt wee then,in that wee ſæ is vayne,
Oz take delight,in that wee pzoue but dzoſſe?
Why glozy wee,oz ſæke for golden gayne?
Sith at the length, wee reape therof but loſſe.
Wæ lothe to leaue,our hutches filde with golde :
Our annual rents,it græues vs to fozgo,
Our buildings bzaue,which glads vs to beholde :
Our pleaſant ſpozt,it græues vs to fozgo.
Wæ nothing bzought,ne ought ſhall carry hence,
Lyfe loſt,behinde goods,mony,land,wæ leaue :
And naked ſhall returne,aſſured whence
Befoze wæ came,when death doth life bereaue :
Liue then, to leaue thy life in euery hower,
Learne how to lead thy minde,from vayne deſire ,
Of filthy dzoſſe,whoſe ſugereſt ſweet is ſower,
When dzeadfull death,ſhall yæld our earthly hire.
What is our wozld but vayne,fraught full of vice,
Wherin wee liue,allured by diſceat :

　　　　　　　M　　　　　　Which

# The gorgious Gallery

Which vs in youth, to error doth entice,
And stirs vs vp, inflamed by follyes heat.
Our mindes are moued, with every fond desire,
Wée gloze in that, the which wée sée vnsure:
Wée vsuall séeke great honor to aspire,
Whose greatest pompe, doth but a while endure:
For proofe the flower, bedea with gorgious hew,
As sone with heate, of scorching sun doth fade:
As doth the wæde, the which vnsæmly grew,
And showes it selfe, vncouerd with the shade.
The stately ship, which floates on seming fluds,
With waue is tost, as sone to surging Seas:
Doth yæld his pompe, though fraught with store of gods,
As vessell weake, whose force the streame assayes:
Our selues may show, the state of eche degrée,
As Sampson stout, whose force Philistians felt:
For wealth, let Diues, glut with golde our Mirror bée,
Marke Nemrods fall, whose hart with pride was swelt.
And diuers mo, whose preter pathes may learne,
Our future steps, our vayn vnsteady stay:
Whose elder lyues, already past may warne,
Vs shun such snares, which leades vs to decay.

### FINIS.        T.P.

## of gallant Inuentions.

### The fall of folly, exampled by needy Age.

Ehold mée here whose youth, to withered yeres,
Doth bow and bend, compeld by crooked age :
Sée here my lyms, whose strength benumbde weres,
Whose pleasure spent, gray heares, bid to bee sags.

But loe to late I lothe my life lewd spent,
And wish in vayne, I had fozeséene in youth :
These dzowsie dayes, which moues mée to lament
My idle youth prou'd, what therof ensueth.

Unstozde olde yeres, must serue foz lusty pzime,
These féebled ioynts, must séeke to serue their want:
With tedious toyle, because I vsde not time,
Loe thus I liue, suffisde perfozce to scant.

In flaunting yeres, I flaunting flozisht fozth,
Amid delight, puft vp, with puffing pzyde :
Meane garments then, I déemed nothing wozth,
Nay, scace the best, might serue, my flesh to hide.

I thought them foes, which tolde mée of my fault,
And iudgd them speake, of rigoz, not good will :
Who toulde of gayne, mée thought foz hire did hault,
Then loe, I lothe what now I wish by skill.

Experience moues mée mone, the moze my gréefe,
In lyuely yeres, because I did not shun
Such idle steps, least voyd of such reléefe,
As might haue helpt my age, now youth is dun.

But what pzeuayles to wish I would I had,
Sith time delayd, may not bée calde agayne :
A guerdon iust, (foz such as youth too bad
Consumes, (it is) in time therfoze take payne.

M ii                                        Seeke

# The gorgious Gallery

Seeke how in youth to serue contented age,
Learne, how to lead, your life in vertues lore :
Beholde you mee, attacht with death his page,
Constraynd through want, my lewdnes to deplore.

What greefe more great, vnto a hauty hart,
Then is distresse, by folly forste to fall :
What care more cruell or lothsom, (to depart
From wealth to want) it greeues vs to the gall.

But what auayles to boast, or vaunt of vayne?
What profit ist, to prayse a passed pryde ?
Sith it consum'd, is but a pinching payne,
A heape of harmes, whose hurt I wretch haue tryde.

A direfull dreed, a surge of sorowing sobs,
A carking care, a mount of messiue mone :
A sacke of sin, coucht full of rankered knobs,
A wauering weed, whose force is sone orethrone.

For profe behold, the boast of breathing breath,
See see how sone, his valiaunst vaunt doth vade :
Our pleasant prime, is subiect vnto death,
By vices brgde, in waues of wo to wade.

I know the state, and trust of euery tyme,
I see the shame, wherto eche vice doth cum :
Therfore (by mee) learne how to leaue such crime,
Fœlix quem faciunt, aliena pericula cautum.

Let mee your Mirror, learne you leaue whats lewd,
My fall forepassed, let teach you to beware :
My auncient yeres with tryall tript, haue bewd,
The vaunt of vice, to be but carking care.

## FINIS.   T.P.

# of gallant Inuentions.

AY mee, ay mee, I sighe to see, the Sythe a fielde.
Downe goeth the Grasse, soone wrought to withered Hay:
Ay mee alas, ay mee alas, that beauty needes must yeeld,
And Princes passe, as Grasse doth fade away.

Ay mee, ay mee, that life cannot haue lasting leaue,
Nor Golde, take holde, of euerlasting ioy:
Ay mee alas, ay mee alas, that time hath talents to receyue,
And yet no time, can make a suer stay.

Ay mee, ay mee, that wit can not haue wished choyce,
Nor wish can win, that will desires to see:
Ay mee alas, ay mee alas, that mirth can promis no reioyce,
Nor study tell, what afterward shalbee.

Ay mee, ay mee, that no sure staffe, is giuen to age,
Nor age can giue, sure wit, that youth will take:
Ay mee alas, ay mee alas, that no counsell wise and sage,
Will shun the show, that all doth marre and make.

Ay mee, ay mee, come time, sheare on, and shake thy Hay,
It is no boote, to baulke thy bitter blowes:
Ay mee alas, ay mee alas, come time, take euery thing away,
For all is thine, bee it good or bad that growes.

### FINIS.

M.iii                                        A

# The gorgious Gallery

## A Mirror of Mortallity.

Hall clammy clay, throws such a gallant gloze,
Must beauty braue, be shrinde in dankish earth :
Shall crawling wormes, deuoure such liuely showes,
(of yong delights.
When valyant corps, shall yæld the latter breath,
Shall pleasure babe, must puffing pride decay :
Shall flesh consume, must thought resigne to clay.
Shall haughty hart, haue hire to his desart,
Must dæpe desire die,  drenchd in direfull dread :
Shall dæds lewd dun, in fine reape bitter smart,
Must each babe, when life shall leaue vs dead :
　Shall Lands remayne: must wealth be left behinde:
　Is sence depriu'd: when flesh in earth is shrinde.
Sæke then to shun, the snares of vayne delight,
Which moues the minde, in youth from vertues lore :
Leaue of the vaunt of pride, and manly might,
Sith all must yæld, when death the flesh shall gore :
　And way these wordes, as sone for to be solde,
　To Market cums, the yonge shæpe as the olde.
No trust in time, our dayes vncertayne bee,
Like as the flower, bedect with splendant hue :
Whose gallant show, sone dride with heat wee see,
Of scorching beames, though late it brauely grew :
　Wæ all must yeeld, the best shall not denye,
　Vnsure is death, yet certayn wee shall dye.
Although a while, we daunt in youthful yeares,
In yonge delightes, wee seeme to liue at rest :
Wee subiect bee, to griefe eche horror feares,
The valiaunst harts, when death doth daunt the brest :
　Then vse thy talent here vnto thee lent,
　That thou mayst well account how it is spent.

FINIS. T.P.

## of gallant Inuentions.

A briefe dialogue between ficknesse
and worldly defire.

¶ Sicknesse.

O darkefome caue, where crawling wozmes remayn,
Thou wozldly wzetch, refigne thy boafting bzeath :
Yæld vp thy pompe, thy cozps muft paffe agayn,
From whence it came, compeld by dzeadfull death.

¶ Wozldly defire.

Oh ficknesse foze, thy paines doo pearce my hart,
Thou meffenger of death, whofe gozyng gripes mee greue :
Permit a while, mæ loth yet to depart
From frænds and goods, which J behinde muft leaue.

¶ Sicknesse.

Ah filly foule, entif'de with wozldly vayne,
As well as thou, thy frænds muft yæld to death :
Though after thee, a while they doo remayne,
They fhall not ftill, continue on the earth.

¶ Wozldly defire.

What muft J then næde, fhzine in gaftly graue?
And leaue what long, J got with tedious toyle :
Pzolong mee yet, and let mee licence haue,
Till elder yæres, to put your Bzutes to foyle.

¶ Sicknesse.

O foolifh man, allurde by lewd delight,
Thy laboz loft, thefe goods they are not thine :
But as (thou hadft) fo others haue like right,
(Of them) when thou, fhalt vp thy bzeath refigne.

¶ Wozldly defire.

Then farewell wozld, the Nurfe of wicked vice,
Adue vile dzoffe which moues mens mindes to ill :
Farewell delights, which did my youth entice,
To ferue as flaue, vnto vnfatiate will.

### FINIS.    T. P.

# The gorgious Gallery

Aeger Diues habet Nummos, sed
non habet ipsum.

He wealthy chuffe, for all his wealth,
Cannot redeeme therby his health :
But must to Graue, for all his store,
Death spareth neither riche nor pore :
Not Cressus wealth, nor Mydas Golde,
The stroke of careles death may holde :
Hee feares no foe, hee spares no freend,
Of euery thing hee is the ende :
Though Diues had great store of pealfe,
Pet still the wretch, did want him selfe.

No Phisickes art, or cunning cure,
May any man of life assure :
No highe estate or beauty braue,
May keepe vs from our carefull graue :
No hauty minde or valyant harte,
Agaynst pale Death, may take our parte :
No curious speach, or witty tale,
Our dyinge corps may counteruayle :
No force, no gyle, no powre or stength,
But death doth onercome at length.

The riche man trusteth in his Gould,
And thinkes that life, is bought and sould :
The sight therof so bleares, his eye,
That hee remembreth not to dye :
Hee hath enough and liues in ioye,
Who dares (thinkes hee) worke mee annoy :
Thus is hee made, to pleasure thrall,
And thinkes that death will neuer call :
Who vnawares with stealing pace,
Doth ende in payne his pleasant race.

The

The greedy Marchant will not spare,
For lukers sake, to lye and sware :
The simple sorte hee can by slight,
Make to beleeue the Crow is white :
No science now, or arte is free,
But that some gyle therin wee see :
Thus euery man for greedy gayne,
Unto himselfe encreaseth payne :
And thinkes the crime to bee but small,
When that they loose both soule and all.

Who lyueth here, that is content,
With such estate as God hath sent :
The hungry Churle, and wealthy Chuffe,
Doth neuer thinke, hee hath enough :
Fortune to many, giues to much,
But few or none, shee maketh riche :
Thus euery man, doth scrape and catch,
And neuer more, for death doo watch :
Who still is present at their side,
And cuts them of, amids their pride.

Such is the world, such is the time,
That eche man striues alofte to clyme :
But when they are in top of all,
In torments great they hedlong fall :
Where they do giue accompt at large,
How they their tallent did discharge :
There no man takes their golden fee,
To plead their case, and set them free :
Then too too late they doo begin,
For to repent their former sinne :

Wherfore I wish that eche degree,
With lotted chaunce content ed bee :

N.                    Lo.

Let not thy treasure make thee prowde,
Nor pouerty bée disalowde:
Remember who doth giue and take,
One God both riche and poore doth make:
Wée nothing had or ought shall haue,
To beare with vs vnto our graue:
But vertuous life which here wée leade,
On our behalfe for grace to plead.

Therfore I say thy lust refrayne,
And séeke not after brickle gayne:
But séeke that wealth, the which will last,
When that this mortall life is past:
In heauen is ioy and pleasure still,
This world is vayne and full of yll:
Vse not so lewd thy worldly pelfe,
So that thou dost forget thy selfe:
Liue in this world as dead in sinne,
And dye in Christ, true life to win.

## FINIS.

Win fame, and keepe it.

Who sées the yll, and séekes to shun the same,
Shall doutlesse win at length immortal fame:
For wisdome, vice and vertue doth perceaue,
Shée vertue takes, but vice shée séekes to leaus.
A wise man knowes the state of each degrée,
The good he praysde, the euill dishonord bée:
Hée sées the good, the euill hee doth espye,
Hée takes the good, the euill hee doth denye:
Hée folowes good, the euill hee doth eschue,
Hée leapes the lake, when others stay to vew:
His honor stands, his fame doth euer last,
Upon the earth when breathing breath is past:

## of gallant Inuentions.

As Solomon whose wisdome recht vnto the lofty skye,
And Dauid King, theyr prayses liue (though bodies tombed lye)
They saw the good, the euill they did eschue,
Their honor liues, the proofe affirmes it true:
Then sithe examples playnly, showes the same,
Their prayses liue, who seekes to merit fame.

finis T. P.

Respice finem.

Loe here the state of euery mortall wight,
See here, the fine, of all their gallant ioyes:
Beholde their pompe, their beauty and delight,
Wherof they vaunt, as safe from all annoyes:
To earth the stout, the prowd, the ritch shall yeeld,
The weake, the meeke, the poore, shall throwded lye
In dampish mould, the stout with Speare and Sheeld
Cannot defend, himselfe when hee shal dye.
The prowdest wight, for all his lyuely showes,
Shall leaue his pompe, cut of by dreadfull death:
The ritch, whose Hutch, with golden Ruddocks flowes,
At lenght shall rest, vncoynd in dampish earth:
By Natures law, wee all are borne to dye,
But where or when, the best vncertayne bee:
No time prefixt, no goods our life shall buye,
Of dreadfull death, no freends shall set vs free.
Wee subiect bee, a thousand wayes to death,
Small sicknesse moues the valiaunts hart to feare:
A litle push bereaues your breathing breath,
Of braue delights, wherto you subiect are:
Your world is vayne, no trust in earth you finde,
Your valyaunst prime, is but a brytle glasse:
Your pleasures vade, your thoughts a puffe of winde,
Your auncient yeres, are but a withered grasse.

Mors omnibus communis.　　finis T. P.

P ij　　　　　　　　　　A

# The gorgious Gallery

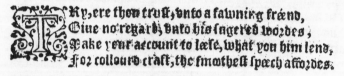

A briefe Caueat, to shun fawning friends.

TRy, ere thou trust, vnto a fawning freend,
Giue no regard, vnto his sugered wordes,
Make your account to leese, what you him lend,
For colloured craft, the smoothest speech affordes.

My selfe haue tried, the trust of tatling tungs
Who paynt their prates, as though they would performe :
(The more my graefe) for they (which) whilome clungs,
Like Bees (goods lost) tole left mee in the storme.

Where I was fayne, in worldly woes to wade,
And seeke releefe, of former freends, no fie :
Perforce constraynd, to seeke my selfe to saue,
Or els vnhelp'd, sance succor still to lye.

I made my mone, the greater was my graefe,
To him which was, as seruant to my state :
But what preuayld, by proofe I found him cheefe,
Who not of mee, but on my wealth did wate.

Donec eris fœlix, multos numerabis amicos,
Temporasi fuerint nubila, solus eris.

FINIS. T.P.

**Beauty is a pleasant pathe to distruction.**

Hrough beauties sugered baites,
Our mindes seduced are :
To filthy lustes to wicked vice,
Whence issueth nought but care.

For hauing tride the troth
And seen the end of it :
What wayle we more with greater greefe,
Then want of better wit,

Because so lewd wee luld,
In that wee see is vayne :
And follow that, the which to late,
Compels vs to complayne.

The boast of Beauties brags,
And gloze of louing lokes :
Seduce mens mindes as fishes are,
Intic'd with bayted hokes.

Who simply thinking too,
Obtayne the pleasant pray :
Doth snatch at it, and witlesse so,
Deuoures her owne decay.

Euen like the mindes of men,
Allurde with beauties bayt :
To heapes of harmes, to carking care,
Are brought, by such deceite.

Lothus by proofe it prou'd,
Perforce I needes must say :
That beauty vnto ruinous end,
Is as a pleasant way.
                    FINIS. T.P.

# The gorgious Gallery

T. P. his Farewell vnto his faythfull
and approoued freend. F. S.

Arewell my fræend, whom fortune forste to fly,
I græue to here, the lucklesse hap thou hast:
But what preuayles, if so it helpe might I,
I would be prest , therof be bold thou maste.

Yet sith time past, may not be calde agayne,
Content thy selfe, let reason thæ perswade:
And hope for ease, to counteruayle thy payne,
Thou art not first, that hath a trespasse made.

Mourne not to much, but rather ioy, because
God hath cut of thy will, ere greater crime:
Wherby thou might, the more incur the lawes,
And beare worse Brutes, seduc'd by wicked prime.

Take hæde, my wordes let teach thæ to be wise,
And learne thee shun, that leades thy minde to ill:
Least bæing warnd, when as experience tries,
Thou waylst to late, the woes, of wicked will.

### FINIS. T. P.

# The Hiſtory of *Pyramus* and *Thisbie*
## truely tranſlated.

IN Babilon a ſtately ſeate, of high and mighty Kinges, (ringes :
Whoſe famous voice of ancient rule, through all the world yet
Two great eſtates did whilom dwell: and places ioyned ſo,
As but one wall eche princely place, deuided other fro : (ſought,
Theſe Nobles two, two children had, for whom Dame Nature
The deepeſt of her ſecret ſkill, or ſhee their byrth had wrought :
For as their yeares in one agreed, and beauty equall ſhone,
In bounty and lyke vertues all, ſo were they there all one.
And as it pleaſed Nature then, the one a ſonne to frame,
So did the glad olde Father like him Pyramus to name :
Th'other a maide, the mother would that ſhee then Thisbie hight,
With no ſmal bliſſe of parents al, who came to ioy the ſight :
I ouerſlip what ſodaine frights, how often feare there was,
And what the care each creature had, ere they did ouerpas :
What paynes enſue, & what the ſtormes in pearced harts y dwel,
And therfore know, what babe & mother whoſe chaſt, & ſubtil brain
No earthly hart, ne when they luſt, no God hath yet withſtand,
Ere ſeuen yeres theſe infants harts, they haue with loue oppreſt :
Though litle know their tender age, what cauſeth their vnreſt,
Yet they poore fooles vntaught to loue, or how to leſſe their payne :
With well contented mindes receiue, and prime of loue ſuſtayne.
No paſtime can they elſwhere finde, but twayn themſelues alone
For other playfeares ſport, God wot, with them is reckend none:
Ioy were to here their prety wordes, and ſweet mamtam to ſee,
And how all day they paſſe the time, till darknes dimmes the ſkye:
But then the heauy cheare they make, when forſt is their farwell
Declares ſuch greefe as none would thinke, in ſo yong breſts could
Ye looke how long, y any let, doth kepe them two a ſunder, (dwelt:
Their mourning harts no ioy may glad, y heuens y paſſeth vnder
And when agayn, they efte repayre, and ioyfull meeting make,
Yet know they not the cauſe therof, ne why their ſorowes ſlake.

With

With sight they feede their fancies then, and more it still desire,
Ye more they haue, nor want they sight of sight they so require:
And thus in tender impe sprong vp, this loue vpstarteth still,
For more their yeres, much more ý flame, ý doth their fancies fill.
And where before their infants age, gaue no suspect at all.
Now nedefull is, with weary eye, to watchfull minde they call:
Their whole estate, & it to guide, in such wise orderly,
As of their secret sweete desires, ill tongues no light espy.
And so they did, but hard God wot, are flames of fire to hide:
Much more to cause a louers hart, within it bounds to finde:
For neither colde, their mindes consent so quench of loue the rage
Nor they at yeres, the least twise seuen, their passions so aswage
But ý to Thisbes Mothers eares, some spark therof were blowen,
Let Mothers iudg her pacience now, til shee ý whole haue knowe.
And so by wily wayes shee wrought, to her no litle care, (snare:
That forth shee found, their whole deuise, and how they were in
Great is her greefe, though smal the cause, if other cause ne were,
For why a meeter match then they, might hap no other where:
But now twene Fathers, though the cause, mine Auctor nothing
Such inward rancor risen is, and so it daily swels. (els,
As hope of freendship to be had, is none (alas) the while,
Ne any loueday to be made, their mallice to begyle: (chere,
Wherfore straight charge, straight giuen is with fathers frowning
That message worde, ne token els, what euer that it were:
Should frō their foe to Thisbee passe, & Pyramus freends likewise,
No lesse expresse commaundement, doo for their sonne deuise.
And yet not thus content alas, eche Father doth ordayne.
A secret watch, and bounde a point, wherin they shall remayne:
Sight is forbid, restrained are wordes, for scalde is all deuise,
That should their poore afflicted mindes, reioyce in any wise:
Though pyning loue, gaue cause before of many carefull yll,
Yet dayly sithe amended all, at least well pleased them still:
But now what depth of deepe distresse, may they indrowned bee,
That now in dayes twise twenty tolde, eche other once shall see.
Curst is their face, so cry they ofte, and happy death they call,
Come death come wished death at once, and rid vs life and all.

And

And where befoze (Dame Kinde) her selfe, did wonder to beholde:
Her highe bequeests within their shape, Dame Beauty did vnfold:
Now doth shee maruel much and say, how faded is that red?
And how is spent that white so pure, it wont to ouerspzed.
Foz now late lusty Piramus, moze fresh then flower in May,
As one forlozne with constant minde, doth seeke his ending day:
Since Thisbe mine is lost sayth hee, I haue no moze to lose,
Wherfoze make speed, thou happy hand, these eyes of mine shall
Abasd is his pzincely port, cast of his regall weeds, (close.
Forsaken are assemblies all, and lothed the foming steed:
No ioy may pearce his pensiue mynde, vnlesse a wofull brest
May ioyed bee, with swarmes of care, in haples hart that rest:
And thus poze Piramus distrest, of humaine succoz all,
Deuoyd to Venus Temple goes, and prostrate downe doth fal:
And there of her, with hart I kozue, and soze tozmented mindes,
Thus askes hee ayd, and of his woes, the Fardell thus vnbindes.

O Great Goddesse, of whose immoztal fire,
    Uertue in Erbe, might neuer quench the flame :
Ne moztall sence, yet to such skill aspire,
As foz loues hurt a medecine once to name :
With what deare pzice, my carefull pyned ghost,
Hath fried this true, and ouer true alas :
My greefeful eyes, that sight hath almost lost,
And brest through darted, with thy golden Mace.
Full well declare, though all that mee beholde,
Are iudges, and wonders of my deadly wo :
But thou alone, mayst helpe therfoze vnfolde,
Els helples ( Lady) streight will kn ap in two
The feeble thzead, yet stayes my lingering life.
Wherfoze, if loue, thy sacred Goddes brest :
Did euer pzesse, oz if most dzeadly griefe,
And causeles not thy inward soule oppzest:
When crooked Vulcane, to your common shame,
Bewzayed of stolen ioyes, thy sw eet delight :

D                                    J

If then I say the feare of further blame,
Caus'd you refrayne your Louers wished sight:
And forst restraynt did equall then impart,
And cause you taste, what payne in loue may bée:
When absence driues, assured hartes to part.

Thy pitty then (O Quéene) now not denye
To mée poore wretch, who féeles no lesse a payne:
If humayne brests, so much as heauenly may:
Haue ruthe on him, who doth to thée complayne,
And onely helpe of thée, doth lowly pray:
Graunt Goddesse mine, thou mayst it vndertake,
At least wise (Lady) ere this life decay:
Graunt I beséeche so happy mée to make,
That yet by worde, I may to her bewray
My wonderous woes: and then if yee so please,
Looke when you lust, let death my body ease.      (man,

THus praying fast, ful fraught with cares, I leaue this wofull
And turne I will to greater gréefe, then minde immagin can:
But who now shall them writ since wit, denayeth the some to
Confusedly in Thisbies brest, that flow aboue the brinke?(thinke,
Not, I for though of mine owne store, I want no woes to write,
Yet lacke I termes and cunning both, them aptly to recite.
For Cúnings clyffe I neuer clombe, nor dranke of Science spring
Ne slept vpon the happy hill, frõ whence Dame Rhetorique rings.
And therfore all, I dœ omit, and wholy them resigne,
To iudgment of such wofull Dames, as in like case hath bin.

This will I tel how Thisbie thus, opprest with dollors all,
Doth finde none ease but day and night, her Pyramus to call:
For lost is sléepe and banisht is, all gladsome lightes delight,
In short of case and euery helpe, eche meane shée hath in spight:
In langor long, this life shée led, till hap as fortune pleased,
To further fates that fast ensue, with her own thought her eased:
For this shée thinkes, what distance may, or mansions bée betwéen
Or where now stands so cruell wall, to part them as is séene
O féeble wit forduld with woe, awake thy wandering thought,
Séeke out, thou shalt assured finde, shall bring thy cares to nought.
                                                                With

## of gallant Inuentions .

With this some hope, nay,as it were a new reuiued minde,
Did promis straight her pensiue hart, immediate helpe to finde :
And forth she fleeres,w̄ swifted pace,ech place she seeks throughout
No stay may let her hasty foote,till all be vewed about.
Wherby at length from all the rest,a wall aloofe that lyes,
And corner wise did buyldings part , with ioyful eye shee spyes :
And scarcely then her pearcing looke, one blinke therof had got,
But that firme hope of good successe,within her fancy shot :
Then fast her eye shee roules about,and fast shee seekes to see,
If any meane may there bee found, her comfort for to bee :
And as her carefull looke shee cast,and euery part aright
Had vewed wel,a litle rifte appeared to her sight,
Which (as it seemed) through the wall,the course the issue had :
Wherwith shee sayd(O happy wall)mayst thou so blist be made,
That yet sometimes within thy bandes,my dere hart Pyramus,
Thou doost possesse if hap so worke,I will assay thee thus.
And from about the heauenly shape,her midle did present
Shee did vnlose heer girdle riche,and pendent therof henf.
And with her fingers long and small,on tipto so shee wrought,
That through the wall to open sight,she hath the pendant brought
That doone shee stayes,and to the wall she closely layes her eare,
To vnderstand if any wight,on th' other side yet were :
And whiles to harken thus shee stands,a wonderous thing behold
Poore Pyramus in Venus Church,that all his minde had tolde,
Performed his vowes and prayers eke, now ended all and dun,
Doth to his Chamber fast returne, with hart right wo begun:
Euen to the same where Thisbie stayd, to see if fortune please,
To smooth her browes and her distresse, with any helpe to ease :
Hee as his wonted vsage was,the Chamber once within,
Lockes fast the doore with fresh complaynts,new sorrow to begin.
But euen lo as his backe hee turned vnto the closed doore,
Aglimpse of light the pendant gaue,his visage iust before:
Let in his face,with speedy pace,and as hee nearer drew,
With wel contented minde forthwith,his Thisbies signe he knew
And when his trembling hand for ioy,the same receyued had,
And hee ten hundreth times it kist,then thus to it hee sayd.

D ij           Though

# The gorgious Gallery

THough many tokens ioyful newes haue set,
And blisse redust, to carefull pyned ghost :
Yet mayst thou sweare, that neuer lyued hee yet.
Who halfe such ease, receiued in pleasure most :
As thou sweete pendant, now in wofull brest
Impersid hast, O happy Pyramus,
Nay beeing a Lady, in whom such ruthe can rest :
Most blissfull Lady, most mighty Venus,
And mighty Thisbie (yea) Venus not displeased,
My Goddesse cheefe, my loue, my life and all :
For who but Thisbie would, nay could haue eased,
A hart remedyles, abandon thrall :
Wherfore since thus ye please, to show your might,
Make mee whole happy, with gladnesse of your sight.

WHiles Pyramus all clad in ioy, thus talkes within the wall,
No lesse content, doth Thisbie stand without and heareth al:
And w̄ those gladsom lightes, where loue doth lightly ioy to play,
And vanquish harts her loue thee bewes in minde somwhat to say
But maydely feare plucks backe ȳ word, dread stops her trimbling
A rosy hew inflames her face, with staine of red among. (tongue,
Yet lo at length her minde shee stayes, her sences doo awake,
And with a sweet soft sounding voyce, this answer doth she make.

Loue Pyramus, more deare to mee then lyfe,
Euen as I first this way, for speech haue found :
Of present death, so let the dreadfull knyfe,
At this instant for euer mee consound :
If ioyfull thought my passing pensiue harte,
Did euer pearse, since parents cruell dome.
Pronounst the sentence, of our common smart,
No deare hart mine, for how alasse may blome :
The fading tree, whose sap deuided is,
Ye, further sweet, I dare with you presume :
Your passed woes, but pastimes ware I wis,
In their respect, that did mee whole consume.
But now sharpe sighes, so stop my willing speeche,
Such streames of teares, doo dim my troubled sight :

And

And inward feare, of parents wrath is such,
Least longer talke, should giue them any light
Of our repayre, that further to recyte,
My heaped yls I neuer dare ne may,
Yet ofte nly, wee wisely beare may meete :
At chosen times which shall vs not bewray,
And this for short, thy Thisbie shalt thou see :
With morning light, here present eft to bee,
To this full fayne would Pyramus, replyed haue agayne,
But part as næde, inforst they must, & as they did ordayne :
Ere mornings dawne they do arise & straight repayre they then
Unto the fore appoynted place, Pyrame thus began.

Myne entyer soule , what prison dollours:
    What hard distresse, and rare deuysed woes:
Of mée thine owne, thy captiue Pyramus,
Haue so sought, this life from bodty to vnlose :
Hard were to tell the tenth, that haue it strained,
With thought hereof, great wonders mée amaze :
How my poore lyfe, the halfe may haue sustayned,
O Thisbie mine owne, whom it only stayes.
And at whose will the fates doo lend mée breath,
Yet may I not the fatall stroke eschew :
Ne scape the dinte of fast pursuing death,
Onles your bounty, present mercy shew :
And this I trust, there may no ielous thought,
Haue any place within my Thisbies brest :
To cause her déeme, I am or may be caught.
With loue but hers wheron my life doth rest,
No bée assured, for yours I onely taste :
Yours was the first, and shall bée first and last,
    Why my most swéet (quoth Thisbie) then agayne:
I doubt not I, but know ye are all true,
Or how may cause of your vndoubted payne :
With her be hyd, who hourely as it grew,
None other felt, but euen what yée haue had :
Yet thinke not swéet, I taste your grefes alone,

Oz make esteeme,as yee of mee haue made,
But ten times moze,if that moze wo begone,
Might euer bee a wzetched maydens bzest,
Where neuer yet,one iot of ioy might rest .
Well then my ioy,(quoth Pyrame)sinze yee please,
With so greater loue,to guerdon my good will :
Safe am I now,but great were mine ease,
If moze at full, I might my fancy fill :
With nearer sight,of your most pleasant face,
Oz if I might, your dayntie fingers straine :
Oz as I wont,your body once embzace,
What say I ease? nay heauen then were my gayne.
Howbeit in vayne, in vayne(ay mee) I waste,
Both wozde and winde, woes mee (alas)therfoze :
Foz neuer shall my hart,O Thisbie taste,
So great an hap,noz neuer shall wee moze :
In folded armes,as wont were to bewzay,
Eche others state,ne neuer get the grace :
Of any ioy,vnlesse wee do assay,
To finde some meane foz other meeting place.
Beholde(alas)this wicked cruell wall,
Whose cursed scyte,denayeth vs perfect sight :
Much moze the hap,of other ease at all.
What if I should by foxce,as well one might :
And yet deserues,it batter flat to ground,
And open so, an issue large to make :
Yet feare I soze,this sooner will redownde,
To our repzoche,if it I vndertake :
As glad I would,then vs to helpe oz ayde,
Sweet hart (quoth shee)wherwith shee stopt his tale :
This standes full yll:to purpose to be made,
And time it askes, to long foz to pzeuayle :
Without suspect,to flat oz batter euen,
Naythlesse, yee this,oz what ye can deuise :
Foz our repayze, by thought that may be dziuen,
Say but the meane, I will none otherwise.

Yet

Yée Thisbie mine, in sooth, and say you so:
(Quoth Pyramus) well then I do you know:
Where king Minus, lyes buried long ago,
Whose auncient Tombe aboue, doth ouergrow
A Mulbery, with braunches making shade,
Of pleasant show, the place right large about:
There if yée please, when sleps hath ouerlade,
And with his might, the Cittie seas'de throughout:
At the same Well, whose siluer streames then runne,
And softe as silke, conserue the tender gréene:
With hue so fresh, as springtied spent and dunne,
No winters wéede, hath power to bée séene:
Without suspect, or feare of foule report,
There goddesse mine, wée salfely may resort.

To this shee said, what shée best thought, and oft and oft agayne,
Was talke renued, but yet at last, for ease of euery payne:
And death to eschue by other meane, who will them not forsake,
At Minus Tombe, euen y same night, they do their méeting make
And so depart, but sore God wot, that day doth them offend,
And though but short his long abode, the feare will neuer end.
And sooner doth not cloake of night, alofte his shadow cast,
But Thisbie mindefull of her loue, and promis lately past
Of fresh new loue, far fiercer flames, that erst her hart opprest,
Shée féelth the force, and this (alas) deuorced stil from rest:
Shée passeth forth in carefull watch, till time haue shapen so,
That slepe wt swéet, soft stealing steps his custome vsage do
And when shée séeth both house and all drownd therin fast & déepe,
With fearful pace & trimbling hand, shée forwards gins to créepe:
Shee gaines the dore, out goeth she then, & neyther far ne neare,
Appeareth wyght saue Phebe fayre, with gladsom seeming cheare
Sole Thisbie ioyfull of this guyde, doth ay I trust it bee,
God lucke thy presence doth import, and bring at last to mée:
More hardyer then before shée did, pronoke her foote to hast,
No obiect giues her cause of let, till shée the towne haue past:
And when shee seeth the pleasant fields in safetie to haue gaynd,
Then ioy therof all dread deuoures, which erst her only payned.

What

What wil ye moze, th'appointed place at length she doth attayne,
Till Fortune please her loue to send, there minding to remayne:
And whiles shæ doth the foūtayn cleare, w thoughtful hope behold
And euery let, her loue may stay, vnto her selfe vnfolde.

A dzeadfull Lyon towne desendes, from Mountaine huge therby,
With thundzing pace, whose sodain sight, whē Thisbie can espy:
No maruel was though terroz then, & straungenes of the sight,
Within a simple maydens bzest, all counsayle put to flight.

Howbeit, though counsayle fayld, yet feare so did ỹ place possesse,
That as the tender bzest, whose age no feare did yet oppzesse:
Now seeth his foe, with rauening Jaw, him ready to receaue,
Sets winges vnto his littell legs, himselfe pooze foole to saue.

Euen so this Mayd, her enemy flæs, vnto a hollow trææ:
For succoz flyes, whose ruthful mone, did succoz not denye: (wilde,
But close her kæpes. The Liones fearce, that in the Mountayns
Deuoured had, new slaughtred beastes, & empty belly filde:
With mossell all embzude with blood, dzawes to the cristal Well,
Hee dzanke, and in his backe returne, this satall hap befell.

Amid this way a kercheife white, which frighted Thisbie had
Let fall by chaunce, as feare and haste, vnto the tree her lad:
This Lion findes, and with his mouth, yet smoaking all in gozes,
And armid pawes it staynes with blood, and all in sunder toze.
That downe a way hee windes, as fier of Hell, oz Vulcans thunder
Blew in his tayle, oz as his corps it seas,d to teare a sunder:

Now Pyramus who could not earst, the wzathfull house fozgo,
Hath past the towne, and as hee dzew the Fountayn neare vnto:
The cloth hee spies, which when (alas) all stained so hee saw,
In sunder toze, the ground about, full trast with Lyons paw:
The Siluer streames with strekes of blood, bespzent and troubled
And there again ỹ cursed trace, the woful pzint to shew:   (new,
A sure belæfe did straight inuade, his ouerlyuing minde,
That there the satall ende (alas) of Thisbie was assinde:
And that her dainty flesh, of beastes a pzay vnmeet was made,
Wherwith distrest with woodlike rage, the wozds he out abzade.

                                                        ¶ The

The lamentacion of Piramus, for the losse
of his Loue Thisbie;

His is the day wherin my irksome life,
And I of lyuely breath, the last shall spend :
Nor death I dread, for fled is feare, care, strife,
Daunger and all, wheron they did depend :
Thisbie is dead, and Pirame at his ende,
For neuer shall reporte hereafter say :
That Pyrame lyu'de, his Lady tane away.
O soueraigne God, what straung outragious woe,
Presents (alas) this corsiue to my hart :
Ah sauage beaste, how durst thy spight vndoe,
Or seeke (woes mee) so perfect loue to part :
O Thisbie mine, that was, and only art,
My liues defence, and I the cause alone :
Of thy decay, and mine eternall mone.
Come Lyon thou, whose rage here only shew,
Aduaunce with speede, and doo mee eke deuoure :
For ruthlesse fact, so shalt thou pitty shew,
And mee (too) heere, within thy brest restore:
Where wee shall rest, togeather euermore.
Ah, since thy corps, thou graues within thy wombe,
Denye mee not sweet beast, the selfesame tombe.
(Alas my ioy) thou parted art from mee,
By far more cruell meane, then wonted fine :
Or common law, of nature doth decree,
And that encreaseth, for woe, this greefe of mine :
Of that beautie only , which was deuine,
And soueraigne most, of all that liued here :
No litle signe, may found be any where,
If the dead corps (alas, did yet remayne :
O great cruelty, O rage of fortune spight,
More greeuous far, then any tongue may fayne :
To reue her life, and in my more despight,
Mee to defraude of that my last delight :

P

Her

Her once t'mbzace, oz yet her visage pale,
To kisse full oft', and as I should bewayle.
But since from mée thou hast the meane outchast,
Of this pooze ioy, thy might I héere defie :
Foz maugre thée, and all the power thou hast,
In Plutoes raigne togeather will wée bée :
And you my loue, since you are dead foz mée,
God reason is, that I foz you agayne :
Receiue no lesse but euen the selfsame payne.
Ah Mulberie, thou witnes of our woe,
Right vnder thée assigned was, the place
Of all our ioy, but thou our common foo,
Consented hast, vnto her death alas :
Of beauty all, that had alone the grace,
And therfoze as the chéefe of others all,
Let men the Tree of deadly woe thée call.
Graunt our great God, foz honoz of thy name,
A guerdoi f the woe, wée shall here haue :
Foz I nill aug Shée dead that rulde thesame,
Pzonounce (O Pluto) from thy hollow Caue :
Where stayes thy raigne, and let this trée receiue,
Such sentence iust, as may a witnesse bée,
Of dollour most, to all that shall it sée.

A Nd with those wozdes, his naked blade bée fierstly frō his sios
Out dzew, & thzough his bzest, it forst wō moztal woūd to glide,
The streames of gozy blood out glush, but hée wō manly hart,
Careles, of death and euery payne, that death could them imparte.
His Thisbies kerchéefe hard bée straines, & kist with stedfast chere
And harder strainde, and ofter kist, as death him dzew moze nere
The Mulberies whose hue befoze, had euer white lo béene,
To blackish collour straight transfozmed, & black ay since are séen.
And Thisbie then who all that while, had kept the hollow trée,
Least hap her Louers long aboad, may sée me him mockt to bée.
Shakes of all feare, and passeth foorth in hope her loue to tell,
What terroz great shée late was in, and wonderous case her fel :

But

But whē she doth approche ÿ tree, whose fruict trāsformed were
Abasht she stands, & musing much, how black they should appere.
Her Pyramus with sighes profound, and broken voyce ÿ plained,
Shee hard:and him a kerchefe saw,how hee hit kist and strained:
Shee neuer drew,but whē the sword,and gaping wound she saw,
The anguish great,shee had therof,her caus'd to ouerthrow
In deadly swoune,and to her selfe shee beeing come agayne,
With pittious playnts,and deadly dole, her loue shee did cōplayne
That owne, shee did her body leane, and on him softly lay,
She kist his face,whose collour fresh,is spent and falne away :
Then to ÿ sword these words she sayth: thou sword of bitter gall,
Thou hast bereaued mee my Loue,my comfort ioy and all.
With that deare blood(woes me)of his thy cursed blade doth shine
Wherfore thinke not thou canst be free,to shed the same of mine,
In life no meane,though wee it sought,vs to assemble could,
Death shall,who hath already his, & mine shall straight vnfolde.
And you O Gods,this last request, for ruthe yet graunt it mee,
That as one death wee should receiue,one Tombe our graue may
With ÿ agayn she oft him kist;& then shee speaketh thus:      (bee,
    O Louer mine,beholde thy loue(alas) my Pyramus.
Yet ere I dye beholde mee once,that comfort not denye,
To her with thee that liu'd and lou'd,and eke with thee will dye.
The Gentilman with this  , and as the lastest throwes of death,
Did pearce full fast at that same stroke,to end both life and breath
The voice hee knows,& euen therwith, castes vp his heauy eyes,
And sees his loue,hee striues to speake,but death at hand denyes.
Yet loue whose might , no t thē was quēcht in spite of death gaue
And causde frō bottō of his hart,these words to pas at lēgth(strēgth
(Alas my loue)and liue ye yet, did not your life define,
By Lyones rage the foe therof, and caus'd that this of mine
Is spent and past,or as I thinke,it is your soule so deare,
That seekes to ioy and honor both,my last aduenture heare.
Euen with that word,a profound sighe, from bottom of his hart,
Out cast his corps and spirit of life, in sunder did depart :
Then Thisbie efte, with shrike so shrill as dynned in the skye,
Swaps down in swoune,shee eft reuiues,& hents ÿ sword hereby.

VVherwith beneath her pap(alas)into her brest shee strake,
Saying thus wtꝭ Isie for him,that thus dyed for my sake :
The purple Skarlet streames downe ran,ꝭ shæ her close doth lay
Unto her loue him kissing still,as life did pyne away.

Lo thus they lou'd and died,and dead,one tombe thē graued there,
And Mulberies in signe of woe , from white to blacke turnde were.

FINIS.

## ☙ The lamentacion of a Gentilwoman
### vpon the death of her late deceased frend
### william Gruffith Gent.

A doutfull, dying, dolefull, Dame,
Not fearing death, nor forcing life :
Nor caring ought for flitting fame,
Emongst such sturdy stormes of strife :
Here doth shee mourne and write her will,
Vpon her liked Louers ende :
Graunt(Muses nyne)your sacred skill,
Helpe to assist your mournfull freend :
Embouldned with your Nimphish ayde,
Shee will not cease,but seeke to singe :
And eke employ her willing head,
Her Gruffithes prayse, with ruthe to ringe.

Ith Poets pen, I dœ not preace to write,
Mineruæs mate, I dœ not boast to bœ :
Parnassus Mount(I speake it for no spite)
Can cure my cursed cares,I playnly sœ :
   For why? my hart contaynes as many woes
   As euer Hector did amongst his foes.

                       Œche

Eche man doth mone, when faythfull frænds bée dead,
And paynt them out, as well as wits do serue :
But I, a Mayde, am forst to vse my head,
To wayle my frénd (whose fayth) did prayse deserue :
  Wit wants to will : alas : no skill I haue,
  Yet must I nédes deplore my Gruffithes graue :
For William, white : for Gruffith, gréene : J wore,
And red, longe since did serue to please my minde :
Now, blacke, I weare, of mée, not vs'd before,
In liew of loue, alas? this losse I finde :
  Now must I leaue, both, White, and Gréene, and Red,
  And wayle my frénd, who is but lately dead.

Yet hurtfull eyes, do bid mée cast away,
In open show, this carefull blacke attyre :
Because it would, my secret loue bewray,
And pay my pate, with hatred for my hyre :
  Though outwardly, I dare not weare thesame,
  Yet in my hart, a web of blacke I frame.

You Ladyes all, that passe not for no payne,
But haue your louers lodged in your laps :
I craue your aydes, to helpe mee mourne amayne,
Perhaps your selues, shall féele such carefull claps :
  Which (God forbid) that any Lady taste,
  Who shall by mee but only learne to waste.

My wits be weake an Epitaphe to write,
Because it doth require a grauer stile :
My phrase doth serue but rudely to recite,
How Louers losse doth pinch mee all this while :
  Who was as prest to dye for Gruffithes sake,
  As Damon, did for Pithias vndertake.

But William had a worldly freend in store,
Who writ his end to small effect (God knowes)
But I. and H. his name did show no more,
Rime Ruffe it is, the common sentence goes,
  It hangs at Pawles as euery man goes by,
  One ryme too low, an other rampes to hye.

Hée prayr'd him out as wozldly fréends dœ vse,
And vttered all the skill that God had sent :
But I: am shée that neuer will refuse,
But as I am, so will I still bée bent :
  No blastes shall blow,my lincked loue awzy,
  Oh: would the Gods,with Gruffith I might dye.

Then had it been that I pœze silly Dame,
Had,had no neede to blot this scratched scroule:
Then Virgins fist,had not set fozth the fame,
How God hath gripte,my Gruffithes sacred soule:
  But wœ is mée, I liue in pinching payne,
  No wight doth know,what sozowes I sustayne.

Unhappy may that dzowsie day bée nam'd,
Wherin I first,possest my vitall bzeath :
And eke I wish,that day that I was fram'd,
In stead of life I had receiued death :
  Then with these woes,I needed not to waste,
  Which now(alas)in euery vayne I taste.

Some Zoylus sot,will thinke it lightlydœne,
Because I mone,my mate,and louer,so
Some Momus match, this scroule will ouerronne,
But loue is lawlesse,euery wight doth know :
  Sith loue doth lend mee such a freendly scope,
  Disdaynfull dogs I may despise(I hope)

Wherfoze I dœ,attempt so much the moze,
By this good hope,to shew my slender arte :
And mourne I must(who)neuer marckt befoze,
What fretting foze dœ holde eche heauy hart :
  But now I see that Gruffithes greedy graue,
  Doth make mee feele, the fits which louers haue.

My mournfull Muse, (good Ladyes)take in wozth,
And spare to speake the wozst,but iudge the best :
Foz this is all,that I dare publish fozth,
The rest recozded is, within my bzest :
  And there is lodg'd, foz euer to remayne,
  Till God doth graunt(by death)to ease my payne.

And

And when that death is come to pay her due,
With all the paynes, that shee can well inuent:
Yet to my Gruffith, will I still be true,
Pay death, holde life, my minde is fully bent:
  Before I will our secret loue disclose,
  To Tantals paynes, my body I dispose.
So liue I shall, when death hath spit her spight,
And Lady (Fame) will spread my prayse I know:
And Cupids knights, will neuer cease to write,
And cause my name, through (Europe) for to flow:
  And they that know what (Cupid) can preuayle,
  Will blesse the ship, that floates with such a sayle.
If I had part of Pallas learned skill,
Or if (Caliope) would lend her ayde:
By trace of time, great volumes I would fill,
My Gruffithes prayse in wayling verse to spread:
  But (I poore I) as I haue sayd before,
  Do wayle, to want, Mineruæs learned lore.
By helpe (I hope) these ragged rymes shall goe,
Entituled as louers lyues should bee:
And scape the chyding chaps of euery foe,
To prayse that man, who was best likte of mee:
  Though death hath shapte, his most vntimely end,
  Yet for his prayse, my tristiue tunes I send.
In hope, the Gods who guide the heauens aboue,
His buryed corps, aliue agayne will make:
And haue remorce of Ladyes lincked loue,
As once they did for good Admetus sake:
  Or change him els, into some flower to weare,
  As erst they did, transforme Narscissus fayre.
So should I then, possesse my former freend,
Restor'd to lyfe, as Alcest was from Hell,
Or els the Gods, some flagrant flower would send,
Which for his sake, I might both weare and smell:
  Which flower, out of my hand shall neuer passe,
  But in my harte, shall haue a sticking place.

But wo is mee, my hart I feare in vayne,
Adue delight: come cursed care:
To bluntish blockes (I see) I do complayne,
And reape but onely sorrow for my share:
  For wel I know that Gods nor sprites can cure,
  The paynes that I for Gruffith doo endure.
Since wayling, no way can remedy mee,
To make an ende, I therfore iudge it best:
And drinke vp all, my sorrow secretly,
And as I can, I will abide the rest:
  And sith I dare not mourne, to open showe,
  With secret sighes and teares, my hart shall flow.
Some busie brayne, perhaps will aske my name,
Disposed much, some tidings for to marke:
That dare I not: for feare of flying fame,
And eke I feare least byting bugs will barke:
  Therfore farewell, and aske no more of mee,
  For (as I am) a Louer will I dye.

## FINIS.